YOUNG MAN, RUMBLE

RYAN SPEAR

Rob,

Wishing you nothing but
the best. All love!

To A-1.

I thank you for equipping me with all the tools that I need. I pray that I use them to be the best me that I can be.

1.1.15

Live Up To It.

I don't have any children of my own yet. However, I am praying that one day I will become a father. My ol' lady (hopefully, my future wife) and I discuss it all of the time. When we would like to have them, how many we want, their genders, how we will raise them, etc. Names are debated daily. Every name that is suggested, the first question posed is, "What is the definition?" No matter how nice a name may sound, if it doesn't have a positive meaning, it is voted down and removed from the list. Naming a human being is a huge responsibility, one that I am looking forward to. I believe that names are very powerful. Announcing yourself as, and answering to something day in and day out can be a gift or a curse. Names often become self-fulfilling prophecies. My parents felt the same way. When choosing my name, they considered a few options. I've heard Lance, Stone, and a couple of others, but they decided on Ryan.

I remember looking up Ryan in the baby name book at the grocery store when I was a young boy. I was happy to see the definition "Strong, Little King." I instantly felt better about myself. I also felt the desire to live up to my name, to live like a King. Not meaning a rich man with a lot of power, but to carry myself in a kingly manner. To be a leader, to live with dignity and honor, to be responsible and dependable, to live with integrity and be courageous, to be strong physically, mentally and spiritually, to make wise decisions, to be a man of my word.

This world has a way of beating you down, and in the process, stealing your desire to be great. Mere existence is the norm. Not too many people truly live to their potential or have the life that they once dreamed about as a kid. We put so much energy into survival that we forget to excel. I felt myself going down that very path. I made a decision. Mediocrity is not an option.

Currently, I am 28 years old. Trying to figure life out. I've had a lot of experiences on this earth, a lot of good times, and some not so great. I have so much to be thankful for. I have great family and friends, an amazing woman by my side, Alexandra (AKA Alex, Al) and her daughter, Charleigh (AKA Bunni, Bun). As I am getting older, and assuming more responsibility, I am not satisfied with life as it is. It has to be more in store for me. I know that it is my duty to create the reality that I want.

When I was a young boy, older guys, like my big brother and his friends, or my uncles and big cousins would tell me to "man up!" They would say this when they felt that I was being childish or behaving less than manly. Now, I am a man. I've evaluated my life and I am not living in a kingly manner. I often hear the terms "man up," "woman up" or "boss up." It is time for me to "King

Up." That is the focus of my life right now, in every aspect. I want to behave like, and carry myself as a King. The way my parents saw fit when they labeled me as such.

1.10.15

Drive Slow Homie.

You never know homie, might meet some hoes homie, you need to pump your brakes and drive slow homie. -Ye

I should've listened to Kanye. I'm not looking to meet any hoes, but I definitely should've drove slow. I got a speeding ticket today. I'm still pissed about it. I woke up this morning and decided that I wanted to take some pictures of the city. I've been into iPhone photography lately, blame it on the gram. I head downtown, blasting the new Nipsey Hussle album at concert levels, feeling good. Doing my typical 75-80 mph on the highway. No, I don't have an appointment, no, I don't have an exact destination. I was headed nowhere fast. I came over a hill, on the other side was a policeman. Radar gun pointed directly at the grill of my jeep. He hit his lights quick, like he was one speeding ticket short of his quota and after this he could take the rest of the month off.

I immediately turned on the dramatics. Before even pulling over, I started shaking my head and hitting the steering wheel as if I was disappointed in myself, trying to get some sympathy. I finally found a spot to pull over, started recording a video on my phone, (just in case things got crazy) and rolled my window down. He asked for my license and insurance, this is the first time in a long time that

4

I've been pulled over with legit paperwork. I handed him my info very carefully, I don't want any problems. I was pulling out all of my manners, trying to get that good warning. He took my info and told me that it would only be a minute. He came back and said that since I've been a gentleman that he knocked a few mph's off of my speed to lower my fine, but that he still had to give me a ticket. I told him that I appreciated that, took the yellow slip, threw it in the glove box, turned my music back up and pulled off.

I got upset about a mile down the road. I just wasted that money and had no reason at all to be in a rush. I'm always in a hurry, even when I'm not headed anywhere. I want everything fast, I need instant satisfaction. I have always had an issue with patience. I hate waiting. I hate slow wifi. I hate slow service. I hate waiting for my girl to finish taking pictures of our food for Instagram before we can eat. I've called myself "working on" my patience for years. Today I decided that I am going to really be mindful of it and try to develop that virtue. It's okay to take things slow. I am going to try to enjoy the next leg of this marathon called life and not rush it. We live in a fast world, but sometimes we really do need to slow down. Life is already short, it's no reason to live it in fast forward. I just wish that I could've thought about all of this before I got that damn ticket.

1.17.15

Ode To Ali.

Dear Champ,

I have many male role models. My father, grandfather, big brother, uncles, big cousins, former coaches, even friends. These are all people that have been very close to me and have had a huge influence on my life. I also have role models that I have never met before. This list ranges from Allen Iverson and Tupac to Job from the Bible. I look up to many great men, they all have had a hand in developing the way that I carry myself and my way of thinking. There is no way that I could ever claim to be self made.

Of all the men that have had a significant impact on my life, other than my father and others that I am very close to personally, no one has influenced me more than you. What you accomplished in the ring, speaks for itself. We all know that you are the greatest to ever wear a pair of boxing gloves. You made sure that we knew it by telling the whole world every time that you got your hands on a microphone. In my opinion, you are also one of the greatest human beings of all time. I have studied you since I was a little boy, and I have always been fascinated. How you spoke with such intelligence and carried yourself with such charisma, your confidence, pride of self, faith, determination, work ethic, how you stood up for what you believed in regardless of the consequence.

I draw so much inspiration from you. Your book, "The Soul of a Butterfly", was the first book that I ever read for pleasure, it gave me my love of reading. I remember the tears (thug tears, they didn't fall) in my eyes as I watched you light the torch at the 96 Olympics. I have your simple, yet genius poem, "Me, We." tattooed on me. I watch your interviews, speeches, and fights, what seems to be weekly. Your words are still as relevant today as they were over 20 years ago.

I pray for your health. I pray that one day your voice will be restored so that the world can hear you speak with that fire again. The disease has had you quiet for a long time now, but I know that you are still thinking. I know that you would have so much to say, however, if that never happens you have already said and done more than enough.

With this being your 73rd birthday, I just wanted to say, thank you. From myself and the millions of others around the world that you have influenced more than you could ever know. On this day, like every other day, it is my goal to accomplish your motto, "Be great, do great things".

HAPPY BIRTHDAY, KING!

1.19.15

M L the K.

"But homie if you change, may you change for the better, back when Martin King had a thing for Coretta, wonder if she seen all the dreams he was dreaming, did she have a clue of all the schemes he was scheming..." - Cole

It's 5:30 AM on MLK day. I'm wide awake. I need to be sleep. I will be getting ready for work soon. I wish that I could stay home and observe, but Dr. King didn't dream of me being broke. The holiday feels a little different this year. With everything going on in the world, it is reminiscent of the civil rights era. People are coming together and protesting in the streets and demanding change, it is a beautiful thing. Selma also was released in theaters a couple of weeks ago, and the film is getting rave reviews. Dr. King is back in the spotlight, exactly where he should be.

I saw Selma with my Pops the first weekend that it came out. I haven't been in a theater that packed since Dreamgirls came out on Christmas Day some years ago (Jimmy got soul). I don't go to the movies often, tickets are too high for me. I ain't paying the five, but I had a feeling that this would be worth the price of admission. The crowd was very diverse, almost every demographic was represented, all here to see the King. I was very excited for the film, I was hoping that it would show how great of a man that Dr. King really was.. I wanted to see more of his story than the usual highlight reel. I'm not going to tell the movie, but to me, they accomplished just that.

I loved watching the relationship between Dr. King and Coretta. In the black community, they are the closest thing that we have to royalty. They are the true representative of black love. A side of their relationship was shown that we usually don't get to see. They were dealing with some real shit. Shit really couldn't get any realer. Being in a relationship, I appreciated this. Here is our hero, the great Dr. King, trying to change the world, dealing with some of the same issues that we all face. At the end of the day, Dr. King was a man, one of the greatest men of all time, but still a man. Coretta was a woman, a phenomenal woman, but still a woman. They were a man and a woman, in love, trying to make it work. She gave him the same silent treatment that I receive, put him in the same dog house that I go to. She got on the same nerves that my girl gets on. Through everything, they remained by each other's side. Even in death. I found it funny that they pointed out the fact that Coretta never remarried. Really? Who wants to come after MLK? You can't find a tougher act to follow. He literally changed the world, how are you possibly gonna impress Coretta? Martin has his own holiday, you ain't Jesus, you ain't Christopher

Columbus, (the only Christopher we acknowledge is still Wallace) you ain't getting with Coretta.

As I write this, my Queen and I are dealing with some real shit. Nowhere near as real as Dr. King and Coretta, nobody is trying to assassinate me, I'm not even eligible to be "assassinated," if anything happened to me, I would just be "killed," but still real shit none the less. This is probably why I woke up almost an hour before my alarm went off. I enjoy this part of our relationship. I love being tested and challenged, and still coming out on top. After we come out of a tough time, we might have a few scars and war wounds, but we're stronger, we have grown. So the tough times don't discourage me, I know that they come with being in a relationship. Every relationship deals with them, even the great Doctor and Coretta. I have a dream that one day our bond will be as strong as the King's.

I just looked at the clock. Got pissed instantly. I gotta get ready for work. I'm taking a nap as soon as I'm free at last.

I don't always understand why certain things happen, but let me find peace knowing that they happen for a reason.

1.23.15

Pray for the Bear.

A few years ago, I received a phone call that I will never forget. It was from my mom. We talk multiple times a day, so this was nothing out of the ordinary. But, when I picked up, my mom and both of my siblings were on the phone. This was not the usual daily check-in.

I could hear it in mom's voice that something wasn't right. I felt my heart rise in my chest. In those split seconds, I thought of everything that could have gone wrong. I was trying to brace myself for what I was about to hear. Did somebody die? Did she lose her job? While my mind was racing, her voice cut through the noise, "I have been diagnosed with breast cancer." My heart dropped.

Like most people, cancer has touched my family before. We have lost a lot at the hands of this terrible disease. This was the last thing that I wanted to hear.

Over the next year, my mom had surgery after surgery. Treatment after treatment. Rough day after rough day. Her belief that she would be healed never wavered. I've never seen anybody have so much faith. I learned so much from watching her battle.

During this time, I was living in Los Angeles. My mother was fighting for her life back in Kansas City. I felt so guilty and selfish being away from her. I felt helpless. She was selfless. She told my sister and me not to move back home, to stay in LA and take care of our business. My big brother was there with her, holding it down.

Though I couldn't be there physically, I still needed to feel like I was helping. I assumed the role of the hypeman. I would send her encouraging texts and voice notes throughout the day, and speak positivity into her whenever I could. "You're too strong, Mama. You're unbreakable." "This is just a minor setback for a major comeback. You're gonna come out of this on top!"

During this time, Kobe Bryant tore his achilles. A lot of people thought that he would never play in the NBA again. They were saying that The Mamba was too old, that this injury is virtually impossible for a player of his age to come back from. He released a heartfelt message regarding the injury and whether or not he would be calling it a career. One sentence stuck with me from his statement, "If you see me in a fight with a bear, pray for the bear." I quickly adopted this adage. Every day I would tell Mom that I was praying for the bear. She had too much fight in her. God is too good. It wasn't her time to go. The bear didn't stand a chance. Through the grace of God, Mom beat the bear. Nine months after that somber phone call, her cancer was in remission.

Unfortunately, my siblings and I were all back on the phone with my mom about a year later. The cancer had returned. We were all devastated. I felt so sorry for my mom, she didn't deserve this.

This time around, she wanted me to come home. I was headed back to Kansas City, I didn't have a plan. I didn't know how long I would stay. I had no clue exactly what I was going to do when I got there. I just knew that my mother needed me, and I needed to be with her this time, for myself.

I've been home for almost two months now. The first couple of weeks, before the doctors came up with the game plan, I was so scared. I didn't know if I was spending my last moments with my mother. When my mind would try to go down a negative path, I would have to talk myself out of it. Mom didn't need any negative energy around her. I'm here to help her fight. The fear is gone, we operate on faith. I know that God is still in control, and we are looking forward to her healing.

Seeing her fight up close has been inspiring. I hate to see my mother dealing with these issues. In pain, taking medication, struggling at times. But witnessing the battle has been so motivating. I know that she is fighting so hard to be here for my siblings and I. To see us continue to grow. With her going through all of this, the least that I can do is live a life that will make her proud. I promise that I will. I will also keep praying for the bear because I know that my mom is gonna kick his ass again. Hopefully, this time for good.

1.25.15

Sunday School.

I was raised in the church. Every Sunday morning growing up, my butt was in a pew. I was not always happy about this, especially when the Chiefs had a big game. Moms didn't care who was on the schedule, we were going to be sitting in the Lord's stadium every Sunday. Service was so long that we would often miss the first three quarters of the game, I was upset almost every week. However, I do have great memories from those days, and I built friendships that I still have to this day. I'm happy that my mother made me go to church and build my spiritual foundation at an early age.

Since I've been an adult, I haven't physically gone to church that often. Joel Osteen is my Pastor. I attend his services on television regularly. I love Joel because he talks about real life and doesn't just try to scare the hell out of you. I appreciate that.

Yesterday, my mom asked me if I would accompany her to church in the morning. She has a new church home, she loves it. It starts at 11, she's walking out of the door by 12:30. I was happy to hear that and glad to go. Praise and worship was jamming. They didn't try to guilt you for offering, things were moving right along. I was enjoying service. It was now time for the pastor to preach.

He preached a message on faith, but what stuck with me was the first thing that he said, "We seem to judge others by their actions and ourselves by our intentions. Great intentions don't mean anything if you don't put them into action." That hit very close to home. Made me really think, and he was absolutely right. I have been working on being accountable and taking responsibilities for my actions, especially being in a relationship. When I was single, I wasn't accountable to anyone but myself, that is no longer the case.

It's always easy to come up with an excuse for why I did something wrong or made a mistake. I have defended certain actions by announcing my intentions, but at the end of the day, we are judged by our actions. Yes, I am human, and we all make mistakes, but mistakes can be avoided. Being human is not a good excuse, I have to tighten up.

The pastor said that if he followed through on all of the intentions that he has in loving his wife that he would be a happier man, this is probably true for all relationships. My actions and intentions need to consistently lineup. Not only in my relationship, but in my friendships, with my family, my work, my relationship with God, in every aspect of life. I'm learning. I'm working on it.

After he finished preaching a great message, the praise team came back and closed the service. I was home, eating and watching the game by 12:45. God is Good.

2.5.15

Two. Five.

Time is flying. I can't believe how fast the days are going by. I feel like I just blinked and missed January. However, it was a relatively productive month for me. I kept my goals in mind and worked towards them. I have no complaints about the first month of the year, but damn it feels like it was only yesterday that Alex and I were in the bed sleep at 11 o'clock on New Year's Eve like somebody's grandparents.

I was riding around (and getting it) today, and I happened to be listening to Joel Osteen's podcast. The topic of today's episode was time. He spoke about how time is more valuable than money and how we need not waste it. This is something that I have agreed with for a long time, but I haven't always lived a life that reflects it. Sometimes I take time for granted, like I know where I can go get some more, but to my knowledge, this is all that we've got.

While I was thinking about time, I had to fill out some paperwork. I wrote the date for the first time today. 2.5. When I was a kid, I used to look forward to this date. This day is exactly 6 months before and after my birthday. This was the day that I could officially add on the big "and a half" to whatever age I was. This was a big deal when I was a kid. I was in such a hurry to be grown.

Only if I knew then what I know now. This grown shit is a setup. Anyway, I remembered how big of a deal this day used to be for me, my "half birthday."

Times have changed, I don't mention the "and a half" anymore when asked my age. Sometimes I really have to think about how old I am. I had to think hard about what I did for my last birthday. Maybe I'm getting old.

I am 28 (and a half) years old, this is crazy to me. I can remember being 16 vividly. My life is completely different than what I pictured it would be at 28. I figured that I would be in my 5th year in the NBA, with millions of dollars in the bank, still macking and hanging, partying from city to city, just living it up. Not happening. But, I am happy. I can still relive my hoop dreams every now and then. I don't have seven figures yet, but I'm working on it. And I've macked, hung and partied with the best of them.

While I am happy, I can't lie and say that getting older is easy on me. I have quarter-life crisis all of the time. I think that I'm not doing enough. I struggle with the fact that I feel like I still haven't found my purpose. I know that time is just going to keep going by faster. I am afraid that I'll wake up one day at 50 and feel as though I haven't been living a meaningful life. It's tough, but lately, I've been doing better. I can drive myself crazy thinking about the future. I understand now, more than ever, that my life is what I make it. I am in control. I can't waste time thinking about what I'm not doing, I have to just do. If I want to live a meaningful, productive life, I have to do meaningful, productive shit. It's quite simple. I have to be who I want to be. I have to live in the present.

I am no longer in crisis mode, I feel really good about where I am in life and where God is taking me. One day soon, I will look up and it will be February 5, 2036 . I know that I will think back to this time and reflect on how fast the years went by. I have to make the most out of them.

2.15.15

I'm Thankful.

I've tried to go back to sleep, but I can't. While I was laying in my bed, my mind started racing. This happens often. The thoughts were very random at first, about what I want to do today, hoping that the snow doesn't come, about the dunk contest last night and the Paddington Bear movie that I saw yesterday with my niece. My mind was all over the place, and then out of nowhere, money popped in my head. I started wondering how much was in my bank account, how I don't have enough, and what I need to do to get more. I felt myself beginning to worry and become stressed.

This past weekend, I met up with my potnas Jordan and Turtle. It was really good to catch up with them. We were teammates in college. I look at both of them as brothers. We were discussing life and how we are going to make it, when Jordan brought up something that was worrying him. My man Turtle cut him off in the middle of his sentence. "There is nothing that wastes the body like worry, and the one who has any faith in God should be ashamed to worry about anything whatsoever." He has been studying Gandhi.

This morning, in the middle of my worry session, I heard Turtle's St. Louis accent pop into my head. I immediately decided to stop worrying. I decided instead to think about how blessed I am. I have so many things to be thankful for. I have my health, I have an awesome family and great friends. I have an amazing woman and little girl that love me to death. My bills are paid, I have a brand new box of Lucky Charms AND milk, I'm good! I have more than enough. God has always been so good to me, and I know that he will continue to be.

He is good, all the time.

These last few months have been some of the toughest months of my life. People close to me and I have been dealing with a lot. It seems like everybody that I know is dealing with something. I guess that's just life. Sometimes it is hard not to worry, and to stay positive. However, I don't have a choice, I know that everything is going to work out how it is supposed to, worrying about something will not change the outcome.

2.23.15

Choose Up.

On this date, two years ago, my life changed. That sounds very dramatic when I read it, but that's exactly what happened. February 23rd is the day that I met Alex, with her fine ass.

I remember parts of this day very clearly. It was a Saturday, another perfect day in Los Angeles. I had two tickets to go see my bro Alec and the Utah Jazz play the Clippers. This was the first NBA game that I ever attended so I was fired up. I decided to take my sister, she's a huge sports fan, so I knew that we would have fun.

We get to the Staples Center, I'm loving the experience. We had great seats, Blake Griffin and Chris Paul were flopping, lil bro was playing a good game, people were drunk in the crowd, it was a great time. Around the 3rd Quarter, I checked my phone. There were more Instagram notifications than usual. I was shocked to see that Alex had been liking and commenting on all of my pictures. I guess I couldn't hide how happy I was because my sister asked me "What are you looking at?!?" she's real nosey, she wanted to know what was taking my attention away from the game. I said nothing, put my phone back in my pocket and watched the action on the court. By this time, my focus was nowhere near that game. I was trying to figure out how the hell Alex found me first of all, and secondly if she was choosing me, or just being nice.

I should probably give some background information at this part of the story. I had been following Alex on social media for about 6 months before this night. She calls it stalking, I say that I just had my eyes on her. I first saw her on Tumblr, I then found her IG and Twitter. I was definitely very intrigued from a distance. When I followed her on Twitter, she gave me a compliment on my locs, I said thank you and gave a compliment back, that was it. That was about three months before this night. I tried to say something to her a month later when she tweeted about one of my favorite books, The Alchemist, but she ignored me. (She denies this happening, but I remember.) As bad as I wanted to reach out to her, I didn't. Pimp-C told me that real players get chose! I really just didn't think that I had a shot. Wasn't gonna have me looking stupid in her DM's hoping for a reply, hell naw. Luckily, God knew that my pride would hold me back and made a way out of no way. She chose me.

I looked back at my phone in the 4th Quarter. I've never been so happy to see a notification. Alex slid right in my DM's. God is good. I knew she had messed up then, all I needed was a toe in the door, and I was gonna kick it down. No way I was letting this opportunity pass me up. I literally used to describe Alex when people would ask me about my dream woman. And now here she was, in my phone. I kept the DM conversation going into the next day. She gave me her number 16 messages later, and she's been stuck with me ever since.

It went down in the DM.

3.9.15

Right Back Ain't Cheating.

For the first time in 3 months, I woke up in my own bed this morning. Sadly, I didn't have the best night of sleep because Alex was hogging the covers. I'm sure that she has a different side of that story, either way, I still managed to wake up feeling refreshed. We just finished a two-day road trip from my hometown of Kansas City back to Maryland. Being on the road together was a fun experience, but we were both over it by our tenth hour on the highway. We'll probably look back on the drive and have great memories, but I'm pretty sure that we won't be doing that again. There aren't enough songs, podcasts, or Instagram videos in the world to entertain us for a 15-hour drive. But, she was a trooper. I just knew that she was gonna end up asking me to drop her off at the nearest airport.

Four years had passed since I'd spent more than a week in my hometown. I moved away in 2011 to live in Los Angeles with my sister. I loved California, I wanted to live there forever. Or so I thought, until I met this fine ass woman that lived in Maryland. I packed up and moved across the country last year to build a life with her.

I didn't expect to ever be back in KC for this long again, but when Mom called, I had to be there for her. I didn't know if I was going to stay for a week or a year, I just needed to be with her.

While I was home, I was reminded of the importance of family. I got to spend quality time with my people. I haven't had the chance to do this as an adult. I was able to hang with Mom every day, I was able to have great conversations with my brother. I went to eat with my Pops every Sunday and talked to him about what it takes to be a man. I was able to kick it with my boys that I haven't got to spend real time with in years. It was great to see how we have all grown from those young boys that used to run the streets into the men that we are today.

Alex also got to come home with me and spend time with my people. We had a great time in my city. We went to the museums, the local shops and she ate some of the best barbecue in the world. She got the full Kansas City experience. I was proud to show her where I come from, she said that she'd never seen anything like KC Pride.

Overall, the last three months have been great for me. Even though it was tough to be away from home for this time, and I wish the circumstances were different, I think that many positives came out of it. Now, I am back and ready to hit the ground running.

Mom's doctors came up with a game plan. She's still fighting, but she doesn't need me in the house anymore. I think she was ready to have her privacy back, so she's good. My relationship is in a great place. God is speaking loud and clear to me, I am very focused. Going home recharged me. Today almost seems like New Year's Day for me, I am getting a fresh start. I am ready to make the most out of it.

3.12.15

Same Ol' G.

While I was back in KC, I was able to hang with some of my good friends, people that I consider to be family. My closest friends are people that I went to high school with. We grew up together and remain extremely close to this day. These people really know me.

It was great to spend time with my folks again, living across the country, I don't get to see them often. No matter how much time passes between us seeing each other, it always feels like the good old days when we link. I know that friendships that have lasted 15+ years are rare, and I do not take them for granted. These are people that I know from experience have my back no matter what. Blood really couldn't make us any closer.

A subject that continued to come up while I was talking to my friends was change. More specifically, me changing. All of the fellas were hanging, just shooting the shit, and we got on the subject of how some people that we grew up with have switched up and are completely different now. No judgment towards them, we were just talking about how much a person can change in a short amount of time. During the conversation, one of my boys looked at me and said, "Shit, you changed." In a lighthearted way. I was shocked, I asked, "How?" He said, "Man you're all settled down now, I never thought I'd see it, you've changed!" I knew what he meant, but I disagreed with him, I told him that I didn't change, I'm still myself, my situation just change. It had to, for me to be the man that I want to be, things had to change. At 28, I can't do the same things that I did at 18. That would be a bad look. However, just because I'm not chasing hoes (his words) or partying every weekend anymore, doesn't mean that who I am, has changed. I look at it as maturing, and I still have a long way to go. I am working on being more productive, living a meaningful life, and trying to find my purpose.

I know that it's crazy for some people to see me in a serious relationship, or practicing Yoga, or reading certain books, or trying to get closer to God, but I am enjoying all of these new experiences. Sometimes I sit and think about how different my life is today than it was a few years ago. Not much is the same, but I remember praying for my life to change. I didn't know exactly what I wanted, but I knew that I wanted things to be different, and they are.

I remember a conversation that I had with my brother a couple of years ago. I told him that if I died right then and there, that a lot of people would remember me by saying, "That boy could shoot a basketball and had some bad bitches." (Again, their words) I want to be remembered for more than that. I want to leave a better legacy than that. So hell, maybe I have changed, if so, I know it's for the better.

3.21.15

On The Right Foot.

This morning, when Alex came home from dropping Bun off at school, she asked if we could talk. I knew that I didn't have a choice, when she wants to have a talk, a talk is had. I immediately thought about what I could have possibly done wrong. I've learned that most of the time when a woman "wants to talk," it's not good news.

But at this moment, she was smiling. I was confused. She sat me down, looked me in the eyes and said, "Babe, I don't care if you can't afford the ring that you want to get me yet. I can just wear a little band. That stuff isn't important." I was relieved that I wasn't heading back to the dog house. However, I didn't feel great about what she was saying. Al is not materialistic at all. She does enjoy nice things, we all do, but she isn't hung up on them. We are both trying to live a somewhat minimalistic life. So, when she tells me that she would like to have something, or that she wants something, I know that she really wants it.

We have been discussing getting married in the Spring. We want to go all in on our commitment. We ain't getting no younger, we might as well do it. We have known that we want to grow old together and hang until we can't hang anymore for a long time. That has been the plan since we first met, we are both comfortable discussing marriage.

We look at rings together often, I know the style that she likes. She doesn't want anything crazy. I'm not Kobe, I don't have 4 million to spend on a ring. She just wants something beautiful, unique, and classy. This is what we have always agreed upon. I'm not going to break the bank, but I want her to be excited when I slide it on her finger. This has always been my plan.

I don't think that she got the response from me that she wanted. I didn't feel relieved, I didn't feel let off the hook. I felt terrible. I don't want to enter our union on that foot. I don't want her to have to lower her expectations and settle. Anybody crazy enough to want to spend their life with me deserves the best. I want to be able to give her everything that she wants.

When I call myself a husband, I feel that it will be my job to provide for my family. I want my wife to know that I can do that. Due to recent events, I am currently not in the position to be the sole provider that I want to be. I need to get my shit together, and I will.

It is nice to know that she is with me because she loves me. I know for a fact that she is not with me for money because she is sticking with me while my ends are barely meeting.

I know that her intentions were well this morning. She thought that I would be happy after the conversation, and I am. She could've easily said that she has run out of patience and that she can't take this anymore. She was trying to be considerate, and I appreciate that. But, I know what I want to bring to the table when I ask her to be my wife. I just can't do that until I meet the expectations that I have for myself. I know what she deserves, and that is what she will get.

Thank you for knowing better for me than I know for myself. I now realize that what I want is not always what I need.

3.29.15

Devil Get Up Off Me.

I drive myself crazy from time to time. For the last two weeks, I have been insane. I know that we are supposed to stay positive and smile through the tough times, know that the sun will come out tomorrow, and that joy comes in the morning and all that, but sometimes that is easier said than done. I'm human. Most days, I am up, but some days, I am down. At times, I am happy being unhappy.

I've been back in the DMV for about 3 weeks now, and I'm looking for a new gig. This shit is so frustrating. Looking for a job and watching your bank account get lower and lower is a terrible feeling. One that I know far too well. In the past, I would deal with these things on my own. I would shut down. I would seclude myself from the world. It would just be me and God, figuring things out. He has always made something happen.

I have a routine. I get in a funk, I'm in a shitty mood and stay to myself and go crazy for a few days. Negativity runs wild in my head, I feel like a failure and that things will never get better. Then, I snap out of it. I remember how God has always looked out for me. Every single time. I start thanking him in advance for looking out for me again, and good things start to happen.

This go around, things have been more intense. Being in a relationship, and living with my girl, I can't go through my regular routine. I can't just shut down and be quiet for a few days. I can't seclude myself. When I do, I hear "What's wrong? What are you thinking about?" And I really rather not talk about it, and now I'm an asshole. So not only am I in a bad mood, but Alex is mad at me because I'm in a bad mood and ruining her good mood. I know that she only wants to help, I appreciate that, but the concept of receiving help and support is new to me. I'm new to all of this. Accepting help and talking about my problems are still hard for me. I like dealing with things my way, on my own. I know this sounds selfish, but that's the only way that I know. I'm an old dog trying to learn new tricks. I'm working on it.

Since I wasn't able to go through my natural routine, this time around, my funk lasted longer than normal. I was really going crazy, saying and thinking all types of negative things. I was so frustrated, I was no fun to be around. I'm sure Alex wanted to put my crazy ass out. She didn't though, she was patient with me, she knew that I was crazy when she first got with me. She's stuck with me now, in too deep.

After a couple of weeks, I decided that enough was enough this morning. I listened to "To Pimp A Butterfly" for about the 100th time, (it's a masterpiece) and decided that I was out of my funk. On the last track of the album, Kendrick asks Tupac how did he manage to keep his sanity, Pac answers, "By my faith in God, by my faith in the game, and by my faith in all good things come to those who stay true." After hearing this, I got on my knees and apologized to God for being so negative and thanked him for every single blessing in my life. Next, I apologized to Alex for being a lunatic. I am officially out of my funk. I know for a fact that God is looking out and that good things are coming my way.

4.15.15

California Love.

Al, Bun, and I, spent the last seven days in California for spring break. This was our first family vacation. We had a great trip. Especially Charleigh, she loved everything about California. She didn't want to come back, probably because she wants to stay as far away from her school as possible. Let her tell it, she doesn't like school, even though she talks about how much fun they have every day when we pick her up. She would rather spend her days at the beach instead of taking care of her first grade business. I can't blame her.

Sometimes, it is still weird to me that I have a family to do stuff like take vacations with. I am definitely experiencing a lot of new things, things that I never imagined. We are all learning and adjusting together. I hope that I am doing a good job of being a family man, I'm definitely learning on the fly, and I'm cool with that. Charleigh loves me, and her Mama is still putting up with me, so I guess I'm doing alright.

It felt good to be back in California for a little bit. I was an LA resident from September 2011 to May 2014. I really enjoyed my time out there. It's definitely my second home. I had great experiences and made good friends. Mostly guys that I used to cook on the basketball court. I saw some of them while I was there this past week. Gave out a few buckets, had to let em know that ain't nothing changed.

Being back in LA definitely made me reminisce. I enjoyed being back and hanging with some of the fellas. I loved being able to spend time with my sister and her husband. I was reminded of a great time in my life. I would play ball every morning and hang with the fellas at the gym. I had a fun job working with some great kids. My weekends were spent on the beach. It seemed like the sun was shining every day, it was hard to stay in a bad mood with that perfect weather. It was definitely a good few years.

My best times in LA came while I was courting Alex. She would come out to visit me, and we would get to run the streets and explore the city together. We went to damn near every vegan restaurant and art gallery out there. We would go to the beach and just sit in the sun and talk for hours. We went hiking and practiced yoga. We would drive by the clubs and laugh at all the baddies waiting to get inside. We have great memories from this time. It feels like that was about twenty years ago now, but it was only two. We will always remember when and where our story began.

I never wanted to leave LA. I loved it there, I still do. I made the decision to move last year when long distance was getting too tough for Al and I. We wanted to be together every day and had to figure out how to make it happen. As much as I wanted to stay, and as bad as she wanted to bring Charleigh out and live in California, we both knew that the timing wasn't right for that. I decided to move to the DMV to take our relationship to another level. I remember when I told people that I was moving to be with my girl. Some thought I was crazy, others thought it was a good move. I really didn't give a damn what anybody thought. I was the one making the decision. I knew what I wanted and what I felt was best for me as a man. I knew that it would not be easy, but I wasn't scared. I was ready for the challenge.

Since the big move, it's definitely been an experience. We've had some tough times, and we've had some amazing times. That's life. No situation is going to be perfect 24/7. It even rains in Southern California, (Tony and nem lied) not often, but it does. I know that I made the right move for me. As much as I miss LA, I wouldn't change my decision. I think that I have learned more about myself and grown more in the past 12 months than ever before.

All in all, it was good to get back out there for a few days. Hopefully, we can make our way back and stay for good soon. I need that sun 350 days a year.

4.20.15

My Lambo's Blue.

This past Friday, I had the most fun that I have had in a long time. I was honored to accompany my lady to the National Poetry Month Celebration at The White House. This was easily one of the best experiences that I've ever had.

When Alex received the email invite from The President and The First Lady about a week ago, she thought that someone was playing a trick on her. After some investigating, we confirmed that the invitation was legit. I was so excited for her, and as her biggest fan, I was not surprised. She deserves to be invited to these types of events. I only had one question at this point... "CAN I COME?" Luckily, they said it was cool for her to bring a +1, and after a background check, (which I was nervous about, even though I knew nothing would come up, I paid big bucks for those expungements) I made the cut!

When I found out that we were officially going, I did what I do every time I get some good news, called Mama. She was so excited! Her first question was, "Will the Obama's be there?" I told her that I wasn't sure, but I was hoping that they would be. I didn't want to get my hopes up. The next thing she said was, "Ask him for a job!"

I think that the POTUS has enough on his plate already, I don't believe that he has time to find a gig for me. We got a good laugh out of that. She was so happy for us. As soon as we got off the phone, she googled the event and sent me a text saying that the President would be opening the ceremony, and the First Lady would be the closing speaker. My hopes were officially up.

The day finally came. I woke up early. It felt like Christmas morning. Alex was laughing at me because I told her that I was wearing my suit. I didn't care, I was told that you could never be overdressed. There was no way in hell that I was gonna be walking the halls of The White House and not be suited and booted. We got dressed and made our way down to 1600 Pennsylvania Ave. We made sure that we got there early, we weren't taking any chances. When we arrived, I quickly noticed that every other man there also wore a suit, I guess I have a little sense.

After we had made it through the line, and all the security checks, we were inside. I was finally stomping with the big dogs. We were walking around in awe. The house was beautiful inside. I needed something to take home, so I went to the bathroom and took some of the fancy paper towels with the President's seal on them. I guess I don't have that much sense after all. After I had eaten about a dozen of the cookies that they were offering, it was time for the event to begin.

We were ushered into a small conference room and seated. I look around the room and still couldn't believe that I was really in The White House. There were around 50 people in attendance, and a good percentage of us were young and black. Everyone was clearly just as excited as we were to be there. Now we were all waiting to see if the Obama's were gonna show.

Our First Lady was introduced. She came out of a side door just as beautiful as she wanted to be. She greeted the room and was seated in the front row. Alex and I could barely stay seated, but we played it cool. A young poet from New Orleans was introduced to open the ceremony. She gave a great speech about the importance of poetry. She concluded her speech by introducing The President of the United States, Barack Obama. The whole room was buzzing as he came out of the side door. He received a standing ovation and made the coolest walk to the podium that I've ever seen. I've met and seen a lot of celebrities and famous people, I've never been star-struck. This was different. I remember exactly how I felt, (and the celebratory gunshots and fireworks at my HBCU) the night that he was elected. I was in shock, Alex and I were both tripping. He was right there! No further than a free throw line length away from us. I've never seen anyone control a room like he did. He gave an awesome speech, (which I can't remember much of because I was too excited to focus) introduced the honoree and his friend, Elizabeth Alexander, and went right back out of the side door that he came in. After Mrs. Alexander had given a fantastic presentation, Mrs. Obama closed out the ceremony. FLOTUS is tough! Everything about her was on point. She gave a great speech about the importance of the arts and made a call to action for everyone in the room to step up and make an impact on the world. After her speech, the celebration was over.

As we walked out, I had a huge smile on my face. I was so inspired. Even though I didn't have the chance to meet the President or the First Lady, just being in the same room as them was amazing. I have never been in the presence of greatness on that level. No matter what people may say about them, they are making history, and that can never be taken away. Just being there made me want to do more. When I saw them in person, it made me realize even more that anything is indeed possible. I will remember this day for the rest of my life. One day, Alex and I will be able to tell our grandkids that we were invited to The White House by the first black President and First Lady. I'm sure by the time that we tell them, the story will change to we met them and I beat President Obama in a game of one on one on his basketball court.

4.27.15

Still I See No Changes.

I have been watching everything going on in Baltimore after the death of Freddie Gray all evening. Another black man dead at the hands of police officers. It hurts. It hurts every time. I see the pain in his family's eyes. That's real pain. A pain that we are feeling far too often.

I remember not too many years ago, I sat at my boy's funeral who had been killed by police bullets. I remember how I felt when those cops were given temporary leave with pay, no other consequences. I remember seeing his father cry at the casket and his baby girl asking where her daddy was. I remember his little brother's face as the person that he looked up to the most was lowered into the ground. I felt helpless.

I feel helpless now. I wish that there was an easy answer as to what we should do as a people. I don't know. How do we change the hearts of men? We say, know, and believe that black lives matter, but some people, in positions of authority, apparently don't agree. It's painful, it's frustrating. This is a fight that has been going on far before our generation became the victims and it does not seem to be getting any better.

I guess all that I can do tonight is hope and pray that things improve. Truthfully, I'm tired of hoping and praying and wishing for justice. I'm sick of our lives being undervalued. I'm tired of seeing new hashtags and t-shirts every month. I wish that I had a solution, a way to make a real change. Unfortunately, tonight I don't. I don't know how to change the hearts of men. I just pray that everybody stays safe. Nothing positive will come from another loss.

5.1.15

Fight Vs. Flight

We are all faced with this dilemma in life. Oftentimes, it is a very tough decision. For men, fighting is often seen as a sign of manhood. We always want to prove how tough we are. However, sometimes knowing when to walk away takes more courage and bravery than fighting. Walking away, or even running away from a situation is necessary at times, but that doesn't always make it an easy task.

My family has always loved fights. It is something that we all have in common. My Mom and Pops used to go to boxing matches before I was even thought of. They passed down their love of the sport to me. Just this past Saturday I was calling both of them asking if they were watching the fights on HBO. We talk almost every day about our excitement for the Mayweather fight this weekend.

When I was young, Pops took it upon himself to teach me how to box, my first lesson somehow ended in me having a bloody nose. He would tell me about different fights that he had went to, fights that he had been in, him fighting for opportunities, and when he and my mom decided to stop fighting and let their marriage go.

Sometimes, you have to throw in the towel.

Pops always gave me this advice, "If you're going to fight, make sure that you fight for something and not over anything. If you fight for something and win, you gain something, if you fight over something, you're just wasting energy." I've always remembered this.

When I talk about fighting, I am not only referring to physical combat. Those days should be over for me, I'm too old to be fighting. I'm still ready though, just in case shit gets outta hand. You never know, I might have one more good rumble for old time sakes. On second thought, I don't have bail money in my budget or health insurance, so I better not.

We often have mental and emotional fights. Life is full of these, we have to fight for our dreams, opportunities and relationships. Nothing comes easy. Not lately, for me at least.

I am now faced with many fights in my life, fighting for my future. I want to be brave enough to fight for something. I also want to be wise enough to know when it's time to walk away. I know that you can't win them all. Fighters are trained to be smart first, brave second. Some never learn that lesson and are too brave for their own good. They think that no matter how much of a beating that they're taking, no matter how many points they are behind on the scorecard, they have to keep going, their hearts won't let them stop fighting. Fight fans classify these fighters as warriors. We love them, even if they don't win. They always believe that they can win, and they are willing to die trying.

I remember a Friday night when I was 19, maybe 20. Me and my boys were at the club, drunk as a gang of skunks. The club just got shut down because a big fight broke out. We weren't in it, but the fight definitely sobered me up a little bit. I was now thinking straight, trying to stay alert. While we were walking to the car, somehow one of my guys exchanged words with another group of fellas. They were more drunk than we were. The words quickly escalated and one of them threw a weak ass punch at my boy. As soon as he did this, a cop's flashlight shined on us and I saw that the cops were out with the dogs. Mind you, we had just been arrested a few weeks before. I really wasn't trying to go through that again, and I definitely didn't want that dog on my ass. So, both groups of us saw the cops and decided to get out of there, we all took off running. The fight wasn't worth it that night, even though I really wish we could've stomped them out.

I'm a man, and sometimes we don't want to do better even though we know better. Sometimes the best thing for us, is the hardest thing for us to do.

When I am faced with the dilemma of Fight vs. Flight, I think to myself, will a victory be worth the effort? Will a loss be worth the scars? If the answers are no, it's time to walk away. If the answers are yes, I'll die fighting for what I believe is meant for me. Well, I'd rather not die, but you know what I'm saying. I'm gonna fight with everything that I've got.

You knew that I would be tested in this life. Thank you for making me unbreakable.

5.14.15

Identity.

For the first twenty-three years of my life, I was a ball player. Well, maybe not the first couple of years, but for as long as I can remember. Ball was life. I played all day, every day. Five on five, three on three, twenty-one, horse, knockout, whatever. When no one else was at the court, I would spend hours working on my game alone. I liked to work at night when I could barely see the rim. I had to rely on the sound of the net to know if I made it or not. Shooting thousands of shots, working on my handle, embarrassing invisible defenders, imagining buzzer beaters. 3....2....1....Swish. The crowd always went wild.

Some of my best memories are of the real games, under the lights, with the stands packed. Girls, gangsters, pretty-boys, cool kids, nerds, and parents would fill the gym. The whole city would be out. If it was a big game and you showed up on time, you were late. No more tickets. Packed to capacity. I loved playing for the crowd. I loved that feeling when I was in the zone and couldn't miss. Watching my defender looking for help. Seeing the coach call a time-out after his game plan was ruined. Pulling up and hitting a deep three on the road to silence the whole gym. There was nothing sweeter. On the hardwood, in front of a packed house, was home for me.

While I was on that court, nothing else mattered. I only had one thing on my mind, one objective, win the game. I was addicted. I was a hoop junkie. I would play sick, hurt, banged up, bruised, it didn't matter. I was a ball player, so if I could walk, I was going to play. If I wasn't playing, I was watching. If I wasn't watching, I was talking about it. I ate, slept and breathed basketball.

Basketball was my first love. I made the decision early in life to wife her. She was the one. I was prepared to spend my life with her. I had it all figured out. After college, I would play pro, have a long playing career, and coach once my playing days were over.

Things did not go as planned. I had a rough college career which included many injuries. I spent way more time than I liked in doctor's offices and on training tables. After five years, three colleges, and four broken bones in my foot later. I was tired. The game left me feeling drained. I still loved her, but I didn't feel like she loved me back. I'm not one to make excuses. I played decent, put up solid numbers, but I hadn't performed well enough to go pro. My playing days were over. I was no longer a ball player.

I was lost. I was so sure that I would always have ball, and now it was out of my life. My goal for about twenty years was to become a pro basketball player. I put in countless hours of work to achieve this, but I came up short. I failed. I didn't know where to go.

However, life couldn't stop, so I had to figure something out.

I graduated college, and for about five years, I had good jobs. I worked with young people, doing work that I could be proud of. I lived in great cities, made a lot of new friends. I fell in love. Life was good. But something was missing. I felt like I didn't have an identity.

When I was young, we used to have to introduce, and say something about ourselves to the class on the first day of school. Every year, I would stand and say, my name is Ryan, and I am a ball player. That was me. That was who I was. This was no longer the case. Without ball, I didn't know who I was. I needed a craft, something to pour my heart into. I didn't feel productive without it.

I felt mute. The basketball court was where I expressed myself. I needed an outlet. After looking in plenty of wrong places, I picked up one of my old vices. A pen.

I've always enjoyed writing. I've always put the thoughts from my head on paper. I would write different experiences that I had, or things that I was dealing with. It was just something that I did. I never put much thought into it. But, when I started writing this time, things were different. I was desperate for expression. I needed a challenge. Something told me to write how I was feeling, what I was dealing with, to get the thoughts out of my head again. When I put the pen to the paper, words flowed onto the page. I felt alive. With the pen in my hand and a blank piece of paper, I felt exactly how I felt with the ball in my hands at the top of the key with my defender on his heels. I was in control. After my first essay, I knew that this was what I had been searching for. I felt free.

My name is Ryan, and I am a writer. I still have my ball player mentality. I want to be the best. The difference is that I don't have a stat sheet or scoreboard to check anymore. I am telling my stories, my experiences, and who can be better at that than me? When I am at my desk finishing up a piece, I feel exactly how I used to feel at the park, alone in the dark, shooting buzzer beaters. 3…..2…..1….SWISH.

6.1.15

Wake Up, Wake Up, Wake Up.

I find myself saying this every month, but I can't believe that it's already June. Time is flying, I feel like I should stop being so surprised by this because it clearly isn't slowing down, ever. I woke up this morning, excited. I have this weird obsession with fresh starts. I am always eager for Mondays. I love the first of every month for the same reason, and because it gives me a reason to play Bone Thugs and rap along mumbling words and acting like I'm in the video. When the first of a month falls on a Monday, I get extra geeked. It makes me want to start all types of challenges. I start thinking that I should read a book every day, or do 10,000 push-ups, or go vegan (until all the BBQ Chicken that I would have to give up crosses my mind), it makes me really want to conquer the next 30 days.

This being the first day of the last month of the first half of the year and a Monday, I was ready for action. This year has thrown some haymakers at me so far, but I'm still here and I'm feeling great. I feel like I'm progressing. The progress isn't coming fast, but a wise man once told me that slow progress is better than no progress.

My plan was to wake up around 6 today and get my day started. I was going to wake up, pray, read, brainstorm, write my goals for the month, workout, shower, eat and get to work on this job hunt. However, I was up later than expected fooling with Alex. I woke up around 7:45, I didn't have time to workout, so that got postponed until tonight. I prayed in bed, just a quick thank you. God said "no problem." I went to the bathroom, I knew that I wasn't gonna have time to read or write out my goals but I did have some time to think in there. While I was sitting, I pulled out my phone and was going through some old notes. This folder is full of randomness. A collection of song lyrics, recipes, old church notes, and other things that I jot down real quick, that I don't use. While scrolling, I saw something that my dad told me about 6 months ago on the phone. "The decisions that you make today, create the reality that you live in tomorrow." I haven't thought about this since I asked him to repeat it so that I could save it. These words really resonated with me that day. I was disappointed in myself when I realized that I forgot all about them. His words were so true, my reality today is definitely the direct result of decisions that I've made so far this year.

Reading this made me think. Instead of making my goals for the month, I decided to make decisions. I've made a lot of goals over the years, reached some, didn't reach others. For me, goals have always been things that I've wanted to do, but they weren't definite, they were almost optional. I was always hopeful that I would accomplish them. But decisions are different, after I make a decision I feel as though it is already so. I've decided to no longer just be hopeful about my life. It's my life. I know what I want from it and how to make those things happen. Now I just have to decide that those things are happening and do them. There are some things that I can not control in my life. I'm not worried about them. I am focused on what I have power over. I started today, on Monday, the first. I wrote out my June Decisions. I will give maximum effort in everything that I do. I will love harder than I have ever loved before. I will stay positive at all times. I will get the most out of every day. I will wake up every morning excited and go to sleep fulfilled. These are not optional. Now it's time to make them happen.

6.21.16

Praise For Pops.

"Any fool with a dick can make a baby, but only a real man can raise his children." -Furious Styles

I just got off the phone with my Pops. I called him early to wish him a Happy Father's Day. I had to beat my siblings to the punch. Petty, I know. I felt bad because I woke him up. I could tell that he was still asleep when I called, he said that he was up all night watching boxing and Game of Thrones. I know he was probably pissed when his phone rang that early, but he played it off.

I told him Happy Father's Day. He replied, "Thanks, son. You, your brother and sister made me a father, so I thank y'all." I laughed and said, "Well you made me, so I sho appreciate you." I told him that I loved him and to go back to sleep, that I would call him later.

That's the type of father he is. Selfless. Even on the day designed to be about him he wants to make it about his kids. He doesn't need to thank us, without us, he would still exist, we wouldn't without him.

One time I asked my dad what he thought his purpose was. He responded quickly, without hesitation, that his purpose was to be a father. He said that he always wanted to be one, that he prayed for a family when he was young. He loves being a Pops. Takes pride in it. He's a good ass Daddy, too. Side note: I think black folks are the only people that still call our daddies, daddy no matter how old we get. I may be wrong, but I've never heard it from anybody else.

I know how blessed I am to have a Pops that wants to be a Pops. We aren't a burden on him. In fact, I think he is his happiest when he's helping one of us. And I've messed up so many times that I've I always kept him happy. He's helped me more than I could ever repay. Whenever I need some advice, he's always got it for me. Sometimes it might not be what I want to hear, but he's always honest. At times, brutally honest. Well, all the time. I love this about him, when I was younger I used to think he was cold. Now I know that he's just not gonna bullshit me. If I ask his opinion, that's exactly what he's gonna give me, whether I like it or not. I've learned that I've gotta have thick skin dealing with Pops. He's been keeping it 100 since before people said keep it 100.

Pops and I are closer now than ever, even though we don't get to see each other that often. My biggest regret being away from Kansas City is that I don't get to see my family on a regular basis. Earlier this year, when I had to go home for three months, I really wanted to make the most of it and spend as much time with my Pops as I could. He's a long distance truck driver and is only home 2 days a week, tops. Every Sunday we would go have breakfast at his favorite soul food restaurant. When we walked in, the staff yelled his name, like Norm in Cheers. For the next hour and a half to two hours, class was in session. We would have great conversations. We talked about everything: these crazy women, religion, raising pit bulls, sports, politics, life, death, and everything in between. Not only did he school me, but he listened as well. This was new. I realized that he was finally seeing me as a man and not a boy. One Sunday, the waitress came up and said, "Can I bring my sons up here so you can talk to them too? Their no good daddy ain't never taught them shit!" We all laughed, but I was thinking, "Hell naw! This is my time, your sons are on their own." She was flirting. Trying to see if Pops would bite. He politely laughed her off and kept talking. These ain't group sessions, these are one on one. Just me and Pops. I will remember the talks that we had over those chicken and waffles forever. Hopefully, we'll be able to have a lot more. Now we talk on the phone a few times a week. That will have to do until I can see him again.

I know how rare it is to have a good father. Most of my friends don't have their dads in their lives. This has been the case since I was young. I've never taken him for granted. I know that he is just doing what he is supposed to do, but a lot of "men" don't do it. My potnas love being around my dad. He talks to them the same way that he talks to me. Gives them the same lessons that I get. He knows that if they don't hear it from him, it's a good chance that they won't hear it at all. They all appreciate him for that, so do I.

I couldn't imagine having a better Pops. He's like Uncle Phil, James Evans, John Q, Mufasa and Dr. Huxtable all in one (not Bill Cosby, Dr. Huxtable). I've learned so much from him. I've received so much. The greatest gift that he's given me has been the example that he's set. After seeing what a great father looks like, I have no excuse. I pray that whenever I get jumped into the daddy gang my son will feel about me the same way that I feel about my Pops.

6.24.15

Know Your Role.

This past Sunday (Father's Day) was laid back for me. Since I live
over 1,000 miles away from my Pops I didn't get to see him, but we
did have a good phone conversation. Alex was out of the country
on business, and Charleigh was with her grandparents. I had the
house to myself. Meaning, classic No Limit records were being
played at bachelor pad levels, draws were not worn at all, the
meals that I ate were not the healthiest, and plenty of naps were
taken. Just a high-quality day.

On Father's Day, I've never been one to call or text every man that
I know that has kids. I feel as though that is their children's
responsibility. I'll call my Pops, and you call yours. Uncles, cousins,
homies, coaches, etc. don't hear from me. This year, I did text my
big brother Jus, since he gave me my only niece and my brother
Joe since he became a first time dad last month. When I told them
Happy Father's Day, they both said it back. This kind of threw me
off, I guess I wasn't expecting it, but I said thank you. I received a
couple of other texts throughout the day, I was thankful for them
all. Especially when Alex finally had wifi and could iMessage me.
Her message meant the most to me. It really made me think.
Monday, I cleaned up the house, put my draws on and went to
grab Al from the airport. After I had picked her up, we went to go

grab Charleigh from summer camp. When we got her, she gave me a huge hug and whispered, "I got you a present for Father's Day." She was so excited. I was too.

When we got back home, she ran to her room and brought out a gift bag. In the bag was a beautiful handmade card, a handmade arrowhead necklace that represents Kansas City and .81 cents. It was so sweet. I felt tears in my eyes, but they didn't come out. This happens a lot when something touches me (when Mufasa died, when Ali lit the torch in Atlanta, when Babyface sang at Martin & Gina's wedding, when Cleo's car got shot up, when Allen Iverson retired, when Will wanted to know how come his Dad didn't want him, man). I gave Charleigh a huge bear hug and kiss on the cheek and told her how much I loved her. She was so happy and proud of her gifts. I put the card on my dresser, dropped the .81 cents back in her piggy bank and haven't taken the necklace off since.

I guess because she isn't my own seed, and since Al & I aren't married yet, I thought that Father's Day didn't apply to me. I still don't look at myself as a father, but I do think that I play a major role in Charleigh's life. That's my girl. I often joke with Alex that if she dumps me, I'm fighting for custody. I love her. I love the role that I play in her life and the relationship that we are forming. I pray that it continues to grow. I learn so much from her every day. I feel honored that she even thought of me on Father's Day.

Last week I was looking at HumansofNY 's Instagram. I saw a picture of a middle-aged man with a young boy. The caption stated, "I'm not his father. I'm his friend" He was asked how they met, his response, "I love his Mother, and it was a package deal." I feel the exact same way about Alex and Charleigh, and it was one hell of a deal.

7.18.15

Looking up.

I'm exhausted. I've never been so happy to be tired in my life. I've been working full time as an Uber driver for about a month now. Initially, I didn't let anyone know that I started driving. I know it's not the most glamorous occupation, and no, it's not my dream career, but it is giving me a way to provide for my family and there is absolutely no shame in that. I was always taught that a man does what he has to do for his family. I was nervous when I first applied to drive, I needed money, but didn't know what I was getting into. It hasn't been bad at all, I've enjoyed doing it. It has many perks, but this isn't a paid uber advertisement, so I'll leave them out. Just know that I like doing it.

When I came back from Kansas City to the DMV, I was very excited. Al and I were in a great place, I was gonna get a good job and everything was gonna be alright. We were ready to conquer the world. Didn't happen. I couldn't get a job. It just wasn't happening. Jobs that I was qualified for wouldn't even give me an interview. It was crazy. I didn't know what was going on. I was extremely frustrated to say the least.

The situation tested us. I felt like shit. I couldn't support my family.

I felt like I wasn't being a man. I never want to feel like I'm being a burden on anyone. Alex didn't make me feel that way, but in my head, that's how I felt. If I'm not being productive, I'm not happy. If I'm not happy, I am no fun to be around. I know that money can't buy you happiness, but when I don't have any, it's hard as hell for me to be happy. It had us thinking that maybe I wasn't supposed to be here. There were times when I came very close to leaving. I was gonna go back to Kansas City where I have connections and work there. Every time it I got ready to leave, I couldn't do it. I knew that my most meaningful connection was here. I knew that we could make it work together, in DC. I know that this is exactly where I'm supposed to be. I believe that it is a part of my purpose.

I had to make something happen. After applying for countless jobs and not hearing anything back, something had to give. I couldn't handle being broke anymore. It was taking a huge toll on me and my family. I signed up to be an Uber driver a few months ago, but I viewed it as a side hustle. I would do it here and there. It was a fun way to help keep my head above water. One day I decided to give it a real shot. I woke up early and drove from 9-5, just like a full time job. When I came home at 5, I had made more money driving than I would've made working 8 hours at my government job that I quit last year. I was hooked. I came home so happy, Alex and Charleigh could feel the difference. My energy was very positive, we all felt better.

Fast forward a month later, I'm driving every day. I am so grateful to be able to work and be productive. I love waking up early in the morning and heading out to work. I love being exhausted at the end of the day. I thank God for every ride that I get. I know that these trips are helping me provide for my family, and that is my primary focus right now.

It's crazy how much better being productive has made me feel. I feel like I am better in every role that I have. I feel closer to God than I've felt in a long time. I'm a better man for Alex. My household is doing great. I am being a better son, brother and friend. My spirits are high. After being low for so long, it feels good. I'm happy that I didn't panic and move home. Things are definitely looking up.

Thank you for treating me better than I deserve. You've blessed me more than could ever be justified. I'm grateful.

7.25.15

Dear Alex.

This is your third birthday in a row that we have spent together. I remember the first like it was yesterday. We had just met in person for the first time the day before. We were in LA. Our journey was just beginning. I wasn't 100% sure that we would get to where we are in our relationship today, but in my gut, I could feel that it was a possibility. It just felt different.

Here we are, two years later. I love you more today than ever. We've been through a lot over the years, but we have come out stronger. We have learned so much about each other. What I have learned to be fact, is that you love me. I never question that.

This being your birthday weekend, I think it's the perfect time for me to say thank you. Thank you for letting me love you, and for loving me back. Sometimes I don't understand why you love me so much, but I'm happy that you do. I feel like you can see things in me that I only thought I saw in myself.

I appreciate you. In our time together, I have had personal ups and downs. It's easy to stick with somebody when they're up, but you learn more about people when you're down. You remain the same no matter the circumstances. You have no idea how much that means to me. We have definitely been tested, and I know that what we have is solid. To quote my mentor Nipsey Hussle, "When confronted with a problem we don't ever flee, we're connected at the bottom like the letter V." Our foundation of friendship will never change. Thank you for being a friend (traveled down the road and back again). I know that you have my back and I hope you know that I've got you covered.

I also thank you for being an inspiration. I know that you inspire people all over the world, literally. But you inspire me the most. I remember having a conversation with one of my boys about you, I was telling him about all of the amazing work that you were doing. He asked me how I felt about it, if I was intimidated. I told him, "Hell no. I couldn't be more proud." I explained how inspirational and powerful it is to wake up with someone that walks in their purpose everyday. Just being able to watch someone manifest their destiny and take control of their own life has let me know that it is possible. I know that you probably don't even realize that you are inspiring me everyday, but you are, and I thank you for that. I love being your number 1 fan. I know that you are just scratching the surface of your greatness and I am so excited to watch you grow.

As I am writing this, you keep asking me if I am finished yet. I guess you're ready to get our day started. I could go on and on but

I'll wrap it up. I hope that you are enjoying your birthday weekend. Thank you for letting me share it with you.

I love you. Always.

7.31.15

IsReal.

People often ask, if you could speak to your younger self, what would you say? This can be a good question to think about. To reflect on where you are compared to where you were, or hoped to one day be. To think about what you did wrong? Or what you wish that you would've done. To think about what you would do differently, knowing what you know now. To think about what you once thought that you knew.

Unfortunately, we can't speak to our younger selves. I don't know of of any time machines, so to my knowledge, we don't get the opportunity to go back and right our wrongs. We must move forward.

Since I've been an adult, I've been working with, and mentoring young men. I've been able to get through to kids that others thought were hopeless. God blessed me with the ability to connect with young kings. Many have listened to advice that I have offered, others have not. I have always tried to have a positive impact on the young life that I have in come in contact with. Whether that be in detention centers, group homes, schools, basketball courts, anywhere that they are. I have formed some great relationships over the years with some amazing young men that will one day be great men. To many of them, I am a mentor or big brother. I fully accept the responsibility that comes along with this. I feel honored when they call me that. But the role that I take the most pride in is, big cousin, specifically to my younger cousin, Isreal.

We have a huge family, literally more of us than I can count. Being in the younger division of my generation, I learned a lot from my older cousins. They put me up on a lot of game. What to do and what not to do. For the most part, I was told to do what they said, not what I saw. I knew that they all wanted what was best for me.

I remember when I was in the 9th grade, my big cousin Jay promised to give me his gold dayton rims when I graduated. I already planned on graduating, but the rims were gonna be a nice bonus. Unfortunately, he didn't get to see that day, he was murdered not too long before I walked across the stage. That loss took a toll on all of us. Wanting to make him and the rest of my family proud fueled me to become the first male in my family to graduate from college. I know that he was looking down and smiling that day.

When I played ball in school, I would always show out when my family was at the game. I wanted them to have bragging rights around the city. They would be in the stands going crazy every

time I got a bucket or crossed somebody up. During my senior
year, my smallest fan was my little cousin, Isreal. He was 5 at the
time, cheering me on at almost every game. When we lost in the
state championship game, I remember how sad he was. I felt
terrible, I felt like I had let him down. Since then, I have always
tried to be a good role model for him, both on, and more
importantly, off the court. Just as my big cousins wanted more for
me, I want more for him.

Now, Isreal is 16, he will be a senior next year. It's crazy how fast
he's grown up. I now look up to him when I see him, he's huge,
still not too big to get whooped though. Living over a thousand
miles away, I am cheering him on from a distance. I am so proud
of him. He's a great young man. He stays out of trouble, helps his
mom out with his younger siblings, does great in school, and is a
better athlete than I ever was.

I make sure to check in on him often. I let him know that I am
here if he needs me. Since I can't go back and give my younger self
advice, it is my big cousin duty to give that to him. Every time that
I talk to him, I encourage him to enjoy these years. Before he
knows it, he'll look up and be damn near 30 like me.

I've thought about which piece of advice I would give my younger
self hypothetically, or advice that I could give Isreal, realistically. It

would be this, challenge everything. Starting with yourself, don't only do what comes easy to you. You might find that you excel at something that you would never try if you refuse to leave your comfort zone. Challenge yourself to be great, don't settle for mediocrity in any area. Challenge your fears, don't let them cripple you, or hold you back. Challenge ideas, figure things out for yourself, don't believe everything that is told to you, especially when it comes to your life. A lot of people will try to cast their doubts on you, because they are afraid to try to do anything special. Don't let them. Do what you want to do. Be your own man. Stand on your own two feet and live the life that you want to live. And if you need help, don't be afraid to ask, especially from me.

I remember when I was Isreal's age, my big cousins were so cool to me. They still are. I wanted to be just like them, they weren't having that. They didn't want me in the streets. They wanted nothing but the best for me, and they made sure that I knew what path to stay on. I respected them for this, and nothing has changed, I still look up to them. They made it very clear to me not to follow in their footsteps, to do better. Now that my role is reversed, I am trying to be a good example. I want my actions to speak even louder than my words. I am trying to raise the bar high. I still see Isreal as that same little boy in the stands. I can't let him down.

Thank you for creating me without limits, give me the courage to live as if I know that this is true.

8.5.15

Eight. Five.

This is my first day as a 29-year-old. Damn. I'm down to my last year in my 20's. Alex has been calling me old all week like she's not right behind me. When I'm 89 and she's 86, I bet the difference won't seem like a lot. But I don't mind, as long as I still have the baby face and get carded everywhere, I'm good. Forever young.

Some years, I have been down around my birthday. I think that's natural. It's crazy. Nobody wants to get old, but nobody wants to die. When you think about it, a birthday is just an annual celebration of not dying for 365 more days. I'm happy to celebrate that. Every day on this side of the grass is a good one.

The girls were out last evening. I had time to think and reflect. I came to the conclusion that life is good. God is good. I'm happy. I'm blessed. In years past, I have made the mistake of comparing myself to others when they were my age or younger. I remember thinking, "damn, Tupac was only 25 when he "died" (yes, I'm still hoping that he will come back one day). Look at how much he did in his short time here. What am I doing?" Or watching NBA players sign 8 figure deals while being years younger than me. Or looking at my friends with law degrees or great careers, thinking that they had their shit together and that I was lost. It is always easy to find someone that you think is doing better than you.

This year, I'm not focusing on anybody else. I'm feeling better than I've ever felt. I am healthy, I am surrounded by love, and all of my needs are met. I'm happy. Today, Al asked me what I wanted for my birthday. I want a lot of random things, (unlike 2 Chainz, he only wanted one thing) but I couldn't really think of anything that I needed. I'm good. I've got a vision of my purpose. Every day I will work to make it my reality. I've got an amazing woman and lil' girl that love my crazy ass and the best family and friends that I could ask for. I'm exactly where I'm supposed to be.

When my boys and I used to work out, preparing for basketball season, we would always push harder on the last set. We would say, "last one, best one." So far, my 20's have been a hell of a ride. I've had some highs and some lows. I've made some decisions that I regret and I've made memories that will last forever. Now I have one more year before I close the book on my 20's. I'm ready for it. Last one, best one.

8.12.15

No Squares.

I don't like to admit when I need help. This is one of my many weaknesses. I can be too strong willed. I think that I can figure everything out on my own. I know that this isn't the case. My pride is my greatest enemy at times.

Sometimes, we are forced to work on our weaknesses. These last couple of months, I've been in a tight spot. I needed a loan, but my pride wouldn't let me ask anyone for help. I kept telling myself, "I got this, I'll figure something out."

My brother Joe called me. I've known him for almost 15 years now. We've been teammates, friend and roommates. We are family. He calls my mother, Mama, and vice versa. We've been through it all together. Good, bad, up, down, legal and otherwise. I trust Joe in any situation. I know for a fact that he has my back. It's safe to say that he knows me pretty well. While we were talking, he could tell that I was stressing. I wasn't complaining, but he knows my current situation. He knows that I don't ask for much, he's the same way. He wasn't gonna wait for me to ask, "You're on bullshit, I'm gonna send you some money bro." Laughing. Not at me, but laughing because he knew that if he asked me if I needed anything that I would say, "Naw bro, I'm good." knowing that I need something. But, since he insisted, I just asked if he was sure, "Yea man, I'm good, if I got it, you got it." I told him, "I appreciate it, you know I'm gonna get it right back to you."

My man Joe is in a great space right now. He plays pro ball, fresh off of leading his team to a championship. Even better than that, he just became a first-time father to a beautiful little girl. He's on top of the world.

I'm so happy for my guy. He deserves all of the good that is coming his way. It would be real easy for me to be envious of him, but that has never been the case. The two of us shared the same dream since we were young guns. We used to look forward to the day that we would get paid to play ball. Countless nights were spent in gyms and on pitch black blacktops working towards that goal. Trying to make it.

I never made it, but he did. When he calls and tells me that he just dropped 30, or that they just won the chip, I'm so proud. I saw the work that he put in day in and day out. I know that he deserves it. Do I wish that I could be right there with him? Hell yes, but clearly, that wasn't in the cards for me.

I've learned a lot from Joe. We've been in a lot of crazy situations together. Some where it looked like it was all bad. He's always kept his cool. He always remained positive, and somehow, we would come out alright.

These are the type of people that I like to surround myself with. When I was young, I would often hear that I need to choose my friends wisely. That always stuck with me. I listen to a lot of life stories, from all types of different people. It isn't uncommon to hear, "All of my friends are dead or in jail." For some, this is just an unfortunate fact, others say this to promote a tough guy image. I'm lucky that for me, this isn't the case. I have some friends that have died, I also have some friends in jail. But, the majority of the people in my inner circle are alive and being very productive. We all could've gone down that path to jail or death. Somehow, we were able to avoid becoming victims of our environment.

Friendship is so valuable to me. Even more so now that I live on the East Coast, and don't get to see my friends often. Our bond is still there. We push each other, hold each other accountable. If i'm bullshitting, I know that one of my boys will check me, and I'll do the same for them. We discuss ideas, plans, and dreams. We laugh, joke and sometimes fight, like all brothers do. We've grown from boys to men. Some have had children, others have had to bury parents. We've been there for each other through it all. God willing, we will continue to be. I hear that you're only as strong as the company that you keep. I hope this is true, because my crew is damn solid. Ain't no snakes in my grass or squares in my circle. Never will be.

8.31.15

Long Live A1.

There was a time when I thought that I couldn't cry. Not like, I had to be a man, and men don't cry. I just figured that I literally couldn't cry anymore. I had dealt with some things that probably should've made me cry. I would be extremely upset and hurt, but the tears never came out. I assumed that maybe my tear ducts were broken. I didn't think much of it. The actual tears weren't necessary, I still felt all of the pain in those situations. I went years without wiping tears from my face.

Recently, this crazy theory of mine has been debunked. I don't cry often. I ain't no punk. However, tears have formed in my eyes and fallen a few times within the past year. All very serious situations, that I have absolutely no shame about.

This week I've been dealing with one of those situations. Last Saturday, I was sitting in the barbershop waiting for Al to get her cut. I noticed that I had three missed calls in the few minutes that I had stopped staring at Instagram and flipped through a GQ magazine. This was odd. I was sitting next to the only person that calls me back to back to back. When I unlocked my phone, I saw that I was tagged in a photo on Instagram. I opened it and saw a picture of one of my best friends, someone that I consider a brother, Richard (Rich for short, AKA A-1, I just call him ONE, for shorter). I was confused. My eyes jumped to the bottom of the caption and I saw the letters RIP. I felt my heart fall to my feet. I couldn't believe what I was reading. I got up and walked out of the shop, Alex followed me. I showed her my phone and she was dejected for me. She had never met A-1, but had heard a lot about him. She tried to console me with a hug. I was in denial, this couldn't be true. I called my brother Joe back. He confirmed the bad news. Somebody stole my brother's life in St. Louis the night before.

Rich was a great guy, a really good dude. Full of life and joy. He had a huge heart. He was a natural leader. ONE wasn't a big guy, but he had the heart of a lion. I never saw him back down from a challenge, on the court or in life. All he cared about was the people that he loved. His woman, his kids, his family and friends. He just wanted to make sure that everybody was taken care of and happy.

I met him in 2007. We were both transferring to Lincoln U to play ball. We played the same position, and would be competing for the same spot. He was from St. Louis, I was from Kansas City, you would think that it might be some friction, but we immediately clicked. We went on to become great friends. We ran in the same crew, BMC. We were brothers, we did everything together. Good and bad. We were as tight as possible. His positive spirit was contagious. I don't remember ever being in a bad mood around ONE no matter what was going on. It didn't matter if we lost a game or won, if we were throwing one of our legendary Blue Magic Monday parties or were getting threatened with being kicked out of school and having our scholarships taken away. Rich was always Rich. After college, we went our separate ways, but our bond was still the same. I knew that we would be brothers for life. I just didn't know that his life would end so early.

This past week has been tough to say the least. ONE has constantly been on my mind. I'll think about a good time that we shared and crack up laughing, then those laughs will turn into tears because I know that we won't make anymore memories. I've been having dreams that we are all together again, ONE is alive and well, we're back running wild, enjoying life. I wake up and it's back to reality. I've called my brothers every day so that we can try to encourage one another. We know that there are no words to make the situation better, but we're all in this together.

When someone close to you dies, people try to console you. They tell you things like, "he's in a better place now" or "everything is gonna be alright." Those statements might apply to older people who have lived a full life. But in this situation, it just doesn't seem true. Rich was 28 years old, a family man. His kids and his woman need him here. Things are not alright. My guy had a lot of life left to live. He had a lot more to give to this world.

While being encouraged this week, I was told that I will get through this. That's true, I will. I've dealt with enough death to understand that life must go on, so I will get through this. But I'm not sure if I will ever get over it. I'm hurting for Rich. I'm upset for his family. Even though I feel so much pain, I can still find joy thinking about the good times that we had. I'm happy that we crossed paths. I am proud to be called your brother. You will continue to live on through me. Salute to my guy Richard Colby Williams. Watch over me. I'm gonna make you proud. I love you, bro.

9.15.15

This Ain't The Honeymoon.

I've learned that most people say that they love all types of music. When I'm driving for Uber, I often ask the passenger what music they would like to listen to. They often say, "it doesn't matter, I love everything." knowing good and well that they don't love the Boosie that I just stopped blasting when I turned on to their nice suburban street.

I enjoy rap, but I've always been an R&B head. I blame it on all of the Midnight Storm on BET and The Quiet Storm on Hot 103 Jamz in Kansas City that I consumed as a kid. I used to fall asleep with R&B playing in the background. I've loved R&B since before I had any business loving R&B. I vividly remember singing Pony word for word with Ginuwine on the radio in the 4th grade. I didn't know what a bachelor was, but you couldn't tell me that I wasn't one and looking for a partner (Someone who knows how to ride. Without even falling off). It didn't matter to me that I didn't know what they were talking about in most of my favorite songs, I just knew that they were jamming. When I got older and knew what they were talking about, my appreciation for a lot of my favorite childhood songs grew.

I remember in my senior year of High School, John Legend's first CD came out, "Get Lifted." One of my favorite songs on the album was "Ordinary People." This is a classic, I loved singing it. I tried to learn how to play it on the piano, but I couldn't get past the intro. It was my shit. Could I relate? Hell no. I was 18 years old and only cared about playing ball and chasing skirts. I wasn't thinking about love. I didn't want to be an ordinary person.

However, now that I'm grown, and in a grown relationship, I believe Ordinary People could be the realest shit ever wrote. I would insert all of the lyrics, but we all know the song. If you don't, the bridge sums it all up.

"I hang up, you call. We rise and we fall. And we feel like just walking away. As our love advances, we take second chances. Though it's not a fantasy, I still want you to stay."

Uncle John knew what he was talking about on this one. This love shit can be hard. There are times when Al and I are completely happy with each other for weeks at a time, but that's not always the case. In the past 7 days, I have received the silent treatment, slept on the couch for 2 nights, kissed and made up, had a great date on our weekly date night, had a fantastic weekend, got back into it on Sunday, went to bed not speaking to each other, talked it out and laughed about it Monday morning, and we're currently doing great again. We ended our night discussing baby names that we will put to use one day. This really ain't a movie naw, no fairytale conclusions y'all. But we aren't confused. We know what we want, and that's why we always work our issues out and get it back right.

This was a crazy week for us. We usually average about 25 amazing days, 3 quiet days and 2 days at each others throats a month. I guess it's becoming our system. It works for us. Though what we have is nowhere near perfect, we are still standing, and growing stronger every day. Sharing a life with someone isn't easy at all, but we are both willing to put the work in.

My Mom has been laughing at us for a week straight. She calls us the craziest little couple she's ever seen. That's her favorite way to describe us, crazy. We very well may be. At least, according to John, we aren't the only ones.

9.28.15

Black Life Matters.

My upbringing was very black. I was raised in a proud black household. I had a huge black family. I spent 8 days a week in a black church. From K-5 to 8th Grade, I went to the black christian school at my church. The school had all black students (well, there was one Mexican student, but he fit right in) all black teachers and administrators. Every month was black history month. In kindergarten, I wrote and performed a rap about Rosa Parks, wearing a kente cloth kufi. The Buffalo Soldiers came to visit the school every year. We would go on field trips to the Negro Leagues and jazz museums. It was a black experience. When I graduated from the 8th Grade, I had a great sense of black pride that has never wavered.

2015 in America has been a crazy year for race relations, just like the other 400 before it. The events of this year have shown that a lot of the issues that people claim are in this country's ugly past, are still alive and very well in the present.

To some degree, many of the challenges that my grandparents and parents faced, I am still facing now. I am blessed that they instilled in me who I am, where I come from and prepared me for what I would deal with in this ugly world.

Now, I have a hand in raising a beautiful little black girl. She's so innocent and full of love. Her upbringing has been a lot different than my own. She has friends and classmates of what seem to be every ethnicity. This is something that I never experienced. I'm sure that it is great to interact with so many different cultures at such a young age. However, as a black child, her experience growing into and being an adult, will be a lot different than most of her friends.

We were recently watching TV together as a family. They were discussing the Freddie Gray case and were showing clips of our people protesting in the streets about an hour from our living room in Baltimore. I could see the confusion on Charleigh's face. She asked, in her soft voice, what was happening. Her mom looked to me, as to say, you've got this one. Thanks. How do I explain 400 years of oppression and injustice to a 7-year-old? How do I explain white supremacy to a child who has never lived in a time where the President wasn't black?

I didn't even know where to start. I didn't want to change every view that she had of this big, safe, friendly world. But, it is my job to prepare her.

I decided that I didn't need to go into too much detail about racism, police brutality, and systematic oppression while she was in her PJ's, getting ready to rest up for another day of second grade in the morning. But I did explain to her how black people have been mistreated since we were brought to this country. I told her that black lives do matter. I told her how we are often hurt by the people who are supposed to serve and protect us, and that the people are protesting in the streets because enough is enough. I explained to her how special she is and why she is so amazing. I explained to her how black is beautiful, and told her to live unapologetically black. I made it clear that she is not better than anyone, but she is also not inferior in any way. That was enough for the night.

As she grows older, our conversations will become more in depth. Hopefully, by the time that she has her own children, and it is time for her to have these conversations with them, things will be better.

After Bun had gone to bed, Al and I continued to talk. We are concerned about Bun's future. We know how cold this world is, and it seems like it's only getting colder. We want to bring other children into this world, what are we getting them into? It's not easy living a black life in America. Never has been. It seems like it never will be. We are hurting as a people. We are tired and frustrated. We have fought, protested, marched, yelled and screamed, but they don't hear us. This system does not agree with us when we say that Black Lives Matter. This has been proven time and time again. It feels like we are running out of options.

I have heard people say that this world is too dangerous. That they would never bring a child into this, that it's not fair. They are too afraid of what could happen to them. I would be lying if I said that these thoughts did not cross my mind. Maybe we would be better off not having another child and being fearful of their future.

I woke up this morning with a realization. We are black. Being crippled by fear is not an option. To be black is to be strong and fearless. It is in our DNA. If we stopped moving forward when we got tired, or frustrated, or felt hopeless, our bloodlines would've died a long time ago. That is not an option. That is not what we do. We didn't give up during the middle passage. Nor during slavery. Nor during Jim Crow. And we won't give up now. We don't die, we multiply. We've gotta keep moving forward, and raising our babies to do the same.

I know that brighter days are coming. I don't know when, but knowing that they are is enough to get me through the darkness.

10.17.15

J-O-B.

I'm writing this at 11:45 PM, Friday. I have the house to myself right now. I spent my night watching the Royals kick ass (shoutout to the home team) and eating a gluttonous amount of chicken wings without any judgment. Aye. Great night.

I want to be asleep, but I am waiting for Al to get in from a concert with her (fast) homegirls. I don't know what made her think that she could be out this late. Curfew around here is usually before the street lights come on, I guess I need to tighten up the ship. She better be walking in the door any minute now, I need to get some rest. I can't do that until she is in the house, safe.

While in bed, I am thinking about how grateful I am. I'm exhausted right now and thanking God that it's Friday. I'm looking forward to getting some rest this weekend. I started a new job last Monday. These last two weeks have been great. This job has taken a lot of stress off of me. I hate having an unstable financial situation. Or in more basic terms, I hate being broke! My prayer was for stability and that has been provided. I am working the hours that I want, in the environment that I want to be in. This is a great step for my family and I. I've prayed for this for months now, and I will not take it for granted.

I am working at the federal heating plant in DC. It's a real cool gig, as far as gigs go. Exactly what I wanted. A place where I can do my work and go home. Once I walk out the door, I don't think about work until I walk back in. I'm working with a great group of guys. Some OG's giving me game about marriage, family and life in general and some young fellas around my age, trying to figure this shit out too. We have a good time every day. I don't wake up every morning dreading going to work, this is a huge plus.

Timing truly is everything. I thought that I was going to be starting this job last October. God clearly had other plans. The past 12 months have been crazy for me. I've had extreme highs and devastating lows. My faith has been tested, but I've never lost it. I have been humbled. I found myself working jobs that I never imagined, working harder than I ever had. I've cried more in the last 12 months than I did in the past 12 years. I've grown closer to Alex and Charleigh. I've learned a lot about myself and what I'm made of. I have seen just how precious and fragile life can be. I've learned a lot of valuable lessons. This time last year, I wasn't in a good place mentally. Now, I know that I am ready for this job to be a stepping stone in my life.

Alex just walked in the house, I'm half asleep writing this, I'll resume this entry in the morning...

It is now 8:30 AM, Saturday morning. It felt great sleeping without having an alarm set. I had a dream that T-Pain was singing at our wedding reception back home in Kansas City. Goals. It was a good ass time, but I woke up right in the middle of "In Love With A Stripper" (she poppin, she rollin, she rollin) because my allergies are whooping my ass this morning.

But let me pick up where I left off, I'm in a great place right now. I feel like I was broke down to my core in the past 12 months, and I have been built back up. I am so excited, not only for the future, but for today. I have a clear vision of what I want my life to look like, and I am getting closer to it. I am humble and hungry, ready to attack life and be who God created me to be. I feel like I'm really starting to understand what life is about, or at least what I want my life to be about. I know that it won't be easy, but I'm up for the challenge. I can't predict what life will throw at me, but I will always roll with the punches and keep moving forward. I'm anxious to see what will come my way next.

11.1.15

Sacrifice.

My day started at 6AM. Earlier than I prefer for a Sunday. Al called me before the sun came up to let me know that she was at her gate. She was waiting for her flight to bring her back to DC from Alabama where she had gone to work for a few days. I was ready for her to come back to me.

Waking up early to a phone call from Alex brought back memories. When we were long distance, she would call and wake me up every morning. It would be around 7 here in DC and 4 where I was, out in LA. I love to sleep, so when I started sacrificing sleep for her, I knew that something serious was going on here. For months, she would ask the same question when I picked up the phone half sleep, "What are you doing?" What do you think I'm doing? Just up, hanging? Playing ball? Partying? You think I got chicks in the living room getting it on and they ain't leaving til 6 in the morning? I'm sleeping! She asked me what I was doing when she called this morning, I told her that I was knocked out, she didn't care, kept on talking. I was trying to stay awake and pay attention but it wasn't happening. I told her that I loved her and that I would be at the airport waiting for her in a few hours.

Other than the early wake up call, this Sunday has been going just the way that I like my Sunday's to go. After I picked Al up, we had a big breakfast, took a great nap, the Chiefs kicked ass, we took some fun pictures, went to the mall, (didn't ball, didn't holla at broads, sorry Pimp C) picked Bun up from her grandparents and came back to the house with a couple of hours to rest before the night game starts. Notice that I only ate once today. Not good for any day, especially a Sunday. Where is Big Mama when you need her?

We were all chilling. Al was editing photos. Charleigh was having a magic show, high off Halloween candy. I was starving. I remembered that I had leftovers from last night. I jumped up, popped my 8 lemon pepper wings and rice in the microwave. I could already taste them. I could've finished all of them last night, but I saved some specifically for this moment. It's not many things in life better than leftovers that you forgot that you had.

I went to take my shoes off, I like to be comfortable when I eat. I hear Alex from the other room, "what are you making, babe?" I'm thinking, "who wants to know?!?" I knew that she was already full, she ate at the mall. I came out of our room and told her that I had some wings left over from last night. As soon as I finished my sentence, I heard the sweetest little voice ask, "can I have some?" Damnit! My thoughts, "did you chip in on these wings?!? " But I'm wrapped around her finger, I made Charleigh a plate, half of my chicken gone, just like that. Sacrifice.

I saw a quote a few weeks ago, "Lust feels like love until it's time to make a sacrifice." Well just today, I've given up sleep and food, this is for damn sure love. Even though I talk shit, and I don't consider these real sacrifices, I do enjoy making all of the real sacrifices needed for our family. I know that they are making me a better man, I wouldn't want it any other way.

It is now after 9, Al and Charleigh are in the kitchen throwing down. I'm watching the game, uninterrupted, waiting on a plate that will be 10x better than my leftovers. Look at God.

11.18.15

Pick Me Up.

I've been off work for the last two days. I just wanted to hang with Al and get some rest. Our only plan was to go check out a museum. Other than that, my schedule was empty. You know, when we break, we break. Word to Bernie Mac. I worked a double shift on Monday, 16 hours, a hot 16, 2/3 of the day, all damn day, too damn long. When I finally got home, I was excited to sleep.

I took a shower as soon as I walked in the door. Al was knocked out by the time that I came to our room. I got in bed, but couldn't fall asleep. Monday was my brother A-1's birthday. Since he passed in August, I've had a lot of restless nights. This was another one of those. He was on my mind heavy. That shit is still crazy to me. It pissed me off that he wasn't somewhere celebrating another year of life.

I fell asleep eventually, when I woke up I was still upset. I didn't feel like doing anything. But, I knew that Alex had been looking forward to going to see the exhibit. I pulled it together and we went. We had a great time at the museum. The artwork was breathtaking. When we left, we were starving. We grabbed some food and headed home. It was nap time.

I woke up in a terrible mood. I just wanted to be alone. That's how I've always dealt with things. Alone. Al woke up and could sense that I was upset. I told her that I wasn't mad at her, I just didn't feel good. She was getting in the shower and I was about to go seclude myself.

I felt dumb when I walked out of the room. First, because I was leaving her as she was getting in the shower, ain't nothing going on in the living room better than that view. Secondly, because I knew that it wasn't fair of me to ruin the whole vibe of the house. When I'm upset, ain't nobody happy. I can ruin everybody's day. I went back in the bathroom. She made me laugh and took my mind off of things. I can never stay upset for too long around her. I can be irritated, I can for damn sure be annoyed, but not upset.

I'm still learning how to be, and have a partner. I'm so used to dealing with shit on my own, that sometimes I forget that I don't have to anymore. Just being close to Alex cheered me up last night. I'm still learning to depend on someone else. It's not easy.

In the middle of the night, I heard a little crying voice in our room. Bunni had a nightmare. We both moved over and let her sleep with us. Those 2 know how to hog a damn bed. I was smashed against the wall. I woke up because I wasn't comfortable. I looked at Charleigh, she was knocked out, sleeping great. She didn't look anything like the little girl that was distraught and wiping her eyes a couple of hours earlier. Just being around her family made her feel better. I've realized that it works for me just the same. I just have to accept it and stop being so damn stubborn, thinking that I don't need anybody. I'm learning.

11.20.15

Step Up.

We just dropped Charleigh off to her father. This is always bittersweet for me. I enjoy the quiet and privacy of being in a childless house. But I miss her being in our home whenever she is away. After about 24 hours, I am always ready for Bun to come back.

I didn't plan on being in this position, raising another man's baby. I didn't give much thought to ever getting married, or being a parent. When I did envision it, I didn't see a blended family as part of the plan. God clearly had a plan of his own.

I fell in love with Alex immediately. Before she ever knew that I existed, I knew who she was, and I knew that she was a single mother. I could've easily kept my distance to avoid the situation. That would've been weak of me. I refused to let the fact that she had a daughter stop me from pursuing who I knew that I was meant to be with.

I've had talks with different guys about blending families. Some express how they don't want anything to do with a single mother. They have no interest in raising another man's child. They have the right to feel this way, it's their life. Everyone knows what they can and can not handle. For me, I had to handle it.

If it wasn't for my father loving, and marrying a single mother, and stepping up to the plate to help raise her son in 1976, I would've never been born ten years later. How could I possibly be scared away by the very action that made it possible for me to be here?

I'd be lying if I said that the situation is never challenging. I can be a very stingy person. I like for what's mine to be mine. I have been forced to work on this. I am not the only male authority figure in Charleigh's life. I am not her daddy. I know this. She was five years old when I met her. She was already an amazing person. Now, I have a hand in raising her. A big hand. But I still know that no matter how many homework assignments that I help with, how many times I go buy medicine when she's sick, how many groceries I buy or bills I pay, how many times I pray with and for her, I will never be her daddy.

For this dynamic to work, I needed a few things to be understood by everybody involved. First, this is my family. Second, I am the only man of this family. I don't share those rights or responsibilities with anyone. Fortunately, that was understood when I got here. Everyone was on the same page.

Being the head of a household was an entirely new role for me. I wasn't scared, but I was nervous. This is not something that I take lightly. I knew that I would have a tremendous impact on a young life. I had to make sure that it was a positive one.

One thing that I learned early in my new role is that, I no longer come first. My needs and wants are secondary. Al and Bun are constantly on my mind. Their needs take priority. I find myself doing things that wouldn't be my first choice with my time. What needs to be done has to get done. It is not an option. If I want to call myself a man, especially the man of our household, I don't have a choice.

I recently had an off day from work. I was fresh off of my second sixteen hour shift in 3 days. I was tired as hell, or as we would say in Kansas City, I was hella tired. Alex was out of the house, she had meetings in the city. Bun was at school. The house was quiet. I was happy. When I was what seemed to be minutes into my after breakfast nap, my phone rang. Alex. She explained to me that Charleigh was sick at school and needed her medicine. Next thing I knew, I was in the jeep headed to the school. I was no longer tired. Duty called.

When I got to the nurse's office, Charleigh was in there trying to look as pitiful as possible. Any opportunity that she has to get out of school, she takes. She asked if I could take her home with me.

Not a chance. I knew that she wasn't that sick. I gave her the meds, loved on her, told her to be tough, made her laugh a few times, kissed her on the cheek and was back in the jeep in 15 minutes.

On my ride back to the house, I had to laugh. I used to hate when my sleep was interrupted. I would have my phone on "do not disturb" during naps. Look at me now. Honestly, I felt great. I enjoy being depended on. When something needed to be done, Al called me. She didn't think twice about it. She called who she was supposed to, the man of the house. I wouldn't want it any other way. While I may not be Charleigh's daddy, and never will be, we still have a very special bond. I will always love her and be here for her. She can always count on that. She can always count on me.

Thank you for putting a vision in my heart. I know that I will one day see it true with my own two eyes.

12.6.15

Just Work.

I am writing this at 7PM on Sunday evening. I got off of work a few hours ago, and just woke up from a nap. This was one of them, I don't even remember falling asleep, where am I, naps. I woke up to check the Chiefs score, we're just about to win our 6th game in a row. I'm fired up. Good Sunday.

When I got off work, I picked Al up from the airport. She'd been out of town since Thursday, working. The house has been so quiet over the past few days. I've been doing a lot of thinking, eating a lot of struggle meals, and taking some good naps. But mostly thinking.

I have always been obsessed with the future, I can't help it. I try to focus on the day and live in the moment, but my future is constantly in the back of my head. My mind has been racing these last few days. Maybe because it is December and 2015 is basically over. It seems like just yesterday we were saying happy new year and now Bun is already writing her Christmas list. Santa said no to the puppy, not gonna have me outside picking up dog shit in the cold. No ma'am. (Side note: The quiet that I have been enjoying over the last few days, is GONE. As I'm writing this, Al is playing her music at hole in the wall strip club levels.) I've been thinking about my life, and where I am. I don't believe in coincidence, I believe that I am exactly where I am supposed to be. However, where I am, is not where I intend to be forever.

I am blessed. I thank God multiple times a day for putting me in the position that I am in. All of my needs are met, and I will never take that for granted. I vividly remember praying to be in the position that I am in now. The position to control my own destiny.

Today at work, I was talking to one of my co-workers about life. We have a lot in common. He's a young king trying to make something happen in this world. We bounce ideas off of each other every day and help each other game plan. We strategize and brainstorm. While I was encouraging him to go after what he wants, I started thinking that I need to take my own damn advice. I've always been able to encourage people, I think that's one of my best qualities. I take pride in being a very positive person, but when it comes to myself, I don't always give that same push.

At times I have been my own worst enemy. For some reason, I've held myself back from attacking my dreams. I know what I want to do, and what I need to do, but for some reason, there is hesitation. The solution is really simple. I've just got to do it. I've got to put the work in. I have no excuse. I want to be better, I need to do better. Across the board— for every role that I play in life.

I've never wanted to be average, but honestly, I've been giving an average effort. Because of this, I have been getting average results. Sometimes it is hard to admit, but it's the truth. To get where I want to be I can't bullshit myself. I can no longer hold myself back or trip myself up. Life already comes with enough obstacles that I won't be able to avoid. I refuse to be responsible for my own failure. I've got to tighten up.

"We can do whatever we want to do with hard work and the ability to make a decision." - Michael Chernow

Straight up.

I made the decision a long time ago that I never wanted to be average. At anything. I can not be afraid of success. I must fulfill my potential. Failure is not an option.

12.23.15

Fill Her Up.

During this time of year, we often hear that it is better to give than to receive. I don't mind doing either. I've always loved to give. However, I also enjoy receiving. I'm still learning how to become better at both.

In the (not so long ago) past, I was incredibly selfish. Especially in my dealings with women. Never being in a relationship before, I was mostly concerned with what I was receiving from the situations.

When I first got with Al, I was trying to figure out how in the hell I was going to do this. I had zero relationship experience. Well, I take that back, I had two "girlfriends" in high school for a total of twelve days. I ended both "relationships" on the sixth day (and rested on the 7th) I just wasn't feeling it.

While trying to figure out how to do this, I decided that I needed some help. I didn't have anybody to really ask for advice. Not too many people that I'm close with have success stories. So, I decided to do some research. I bought a book, The Five Love Languages by Gary Chapman.

In the book he talks about how different people speak different love languages. According to Chapman, a person's love language needs to be spoken for them to be satisfied. The five love languages are: Words of Affirmation, Physical Touch, Receiving Gifts, Quality Time and Acts of Service. I feel like I need 4 out of the 5. I'm greedy (receiving gifts doesn't do that much for me). I enjoyed the book and felt like I learned a lot about myself. But I was reading with a selfish mind. I was thinking about what I needed to receive and not what I needed to give.

The book was a great read, I recommend it, but experience is the best teacher. One thing that I've learned from being with Al, is that our love has seasons. There have been times when we are both doing great, and everything is all good. There have been times that I have been weak and I need her to pick me up. There are also times when she needs me to pour into her more and love on her as much as possible.

Right now, we are definitely in a season where I need to give. I embrace this season. I'm focused on giving. I've learned that the more love that I pour into her, the more love that I see flow out of her. The happier she is, the happier I am. Plus, the more love that I deposit into her, the more I get in return, and I'm still greedy. I need all mine.

Just as I had to learn how to give the love and support that she needs, Al also had to learn how to receive it. It didn't matter how much I was offering, if her heart wasn't open, I was only wearing myself out. Even when she was new to accepting, and didn't always know how, I never stopped offering my love. The more consistent I was, the more trustworthy she became. She feels safe with me now. She knows that the love that I give her is unconditional and hers to keep.

I pray that she continues to feel comfortable letting me pick her up. She's so independent, and because of experience, it isn't always natural for her to receive love. Never the less, she accepts it from me, and as long as she does, I won't stop giving it.

12.25.15

Double Time.

"Keep grinding boy, your life can change in one year. And even when it's dark out, the sun is shining somewhere." -Cole

I am writing this at 10:30 on Christmas morning. At work. I wish that I could be home with the family, but I'll be back with them in a few hours. Bun's face is glued to her new ipad anyway. Al and I will celebrate tonight.

Since I had to be at work at 8, I woke the girls up at 6 to celebrate early and open our presents. Bun jumped out of bed. I didn't have to tell her twice. Al was moving a little slower, but she joined us.

This was my first time being on this end of Christmas. Seeing how happy Bun was opening her gifts made me understand what my parents felt about 20 years ago. I can't even explain how good it felt. My parents made sure that we knew the true meaning of Christmas (cues Jesus is the Reason for the Season). They also did whatever it took to make sure that we had a great Christmas, and we knew better than to ask for too much, so we were always happy.

This time last year, I was away from the girls. I was back in Kansas

City. My Mom was just starting her second bout with cancer and I was praying and believing that it wouldn't be her last Christmas with us. Al and I were in a not so great place. I was out of work and didn't feel productive at all. I was down but for damn sure wasn't out. I knew that I had to stay positive, keep my faith, and understand that what was going to be, would be.

Fast forward a year later, I'm back in the DMV. I spent my first Christmas morning with the girls. I just got off the phone with Mom, she's still pushing strong. She's not going anywhere anytime soon.

Whenever I tell someone that I'm working on Christmas, they say something along the lines of, "Damn, that ain't right." or "That's not fair." I'm happy to be here. I prayed too hard for a job that I enjoy, to complain when I've got to work. I've gotta do what I've gotta do. And I had to get this holiday pay. If Bun was waiting on Santa to bring her gifts, she would've came up short. I can't have that, so I'm here. Hardly working. Listening to Motown Christmas songs on repeat. God is good.

1.3.16

Nothing Was The Same.

Life changed today. I learned that I will soon start my most important job. I found out that I will be a father. Let me say that again, I found out that I will be a father! I just got chills when I wrote that.

I knew that 2016 would be a huge year for me, personally and for the family. However, I didn't know that it would be this big. Life will never be the same. God is blessing us with a child, and trusting us with him (I'm already claiming a son). We won't let him down.

Honestly, it all feels like a dream, but this is real life. I can't completely wrap my head around it yet. I just know that I am extremely excited.

I've known for years now that I've wanted Al to be the mother of my child. We've been trying for almost a year. No luck. We didn't know what the issue was. Alex had tests done and everything came back normal. Since she had Charleigh, we wondered if I had an issue. I took tests. The reports weren't what we wanted to hear. There was good news and bad news. The good news was that I did have soldiers, the bad news was that I have a lower number of strong soldiers ready for action than they like to see. This was shitty news to receive. This probably explains why I never had any real scares when I was out running wild. I'm grateful for that. But now, it's holding me back, it's holding our family back.

After we received the test results, we took a break from actively trying and I started taking vitamins to try to help the cause. The process of trying to conceive had taken a toll on us, we were tired. Getting our hopes up every month, only to be disappointed, had drained us emotionally. As a man, I felt terrible. I couldn't give Alex what we both so desperately wanted. My pride was hurt, it's tough to accept the fact that my body is the source of the pain that we are feeling. We were exhausted. We stopped calculating times and dates, we needed a break.

While on break from trying, we got into a huge fight. It was ugly. Alex went to stay at a hotel for a few nights, we didn't want to be around each other. After three days of no communication, we decided that we should talk about the issue. Us talking led to us making up. That night of making up gave us our first positive pregnancy test. Life is crazy.

I'm still in shock. I'm gonna be a daddy. I feel like Martin when they thought that Gina was pregnant. I want to yell it so the whole neighborhood can hear me. Woo woo woo. God is great.

2.20.16

180.

Before my relationship, I was my only responsibility. I was living in Los Angeles, with my sister and brother in law. I worked as a counselor at a group home. It didn't pay much, but I enjoyed the work. I played ball and hung out with the fellas at the gym daily. I would ride my bike through the streets at night, and along the beach on the weekends. I thought that I was living the good life. It was enjoyable, however, I wasn't making any progress. I slipped into a very dangerous place. I got comfortable. I was comfortable living a very average, mediocre life. I was settling. I was not taking any risks. I was not bettering myself.

Financially, ends were barely meeting, but I was making it, so I was cool with that. I was going in with my sister and brother on the rent and bills. I had no plan to get my own place and definitely didn't have any interest in ownership. I didn't have any health insurance, when I broke my foot playing ball, I couldn't even get it checked out. I had to let it heal on its own. I'm pretty sure that it is still damaged to this day. I never got the tags on my car switched over from Missouri to California. I didn't have car insurance. I was riding like Chamillionaire and Krayzie Bone in 2005. My heart would start racing every time that I saw a cop. I would have to duck off to a side street until the coast was clear. Looking back, this was a pathetic way to live. But at the time, I was content. It just was what it was. I didn't notice anything wrong.

Fast forward almost three years, and a move across the country later. I have made a complete 180. I'm fully insured, I'm blessed to have a decent paying job, and Al and I are looking into buying a house.

This has not been an easy transition for me. The two of us were raised very differently. Alex was taught about financial security, and how to plan well for the future. I was taught how to survive. In my head, as long as I was making it, I was good. This mindset was fine when I was single, I was the only one being affected. My mentality had to change for me to become the family man that I wanted to be.

I remember when I first called my Pops to tell him that I fell in love and was getting out of the game. I was nervous. He has been married and divorced, twice. He doesn't always have the most encouraging opinion on relationships. To my surprise, he was ecstatic. He told me that I would become a man when I had a family. That having that responsibility will be the best thing that has ever happened to me.

He was right. There are times when I find myself out of my comfort zone. Like when I have to pay my health insurance premium, knowing that I will barely use it because my mother has trained me to only go to doctors if I'm on my deathbed. Or, when I have to pay off old debts to get my credit score up. Or, when I have to add more money to savings, and less to checking. I'm still getting used to being a family man. My decisions now impact three people instead of one. Long gone are the days when a burger and fries could feed my whole family. I now have to make all of my decisions with the girls in mind.

I am working hard to grow out of survival mode. I am no longer satisfied, or comfortable barely getting by. I want more. My family deserves more. God wants me to have more. I will have more.

Let me remain faithful in every loss and grateful in every victory.

3.9.16

Cold Winter.

I am at home, alone, in a good ass mood. I'm feeling great because the sun is finally back out in the DMV. There were times this winter that I wasn't sure that it would ever return. Today it was 81 degrees and sunny. Look at God. I hope that spring is here to stay, this winter was tough in more ways than one.

I'll never forget the smile on Al's face on that early January morning. Her cheeks were covered in tears of joy, she was holding up a pregnancy test with two positive lines to the camera on her phone. I told her not to take the test without me, but I guess that she couldn't help herself when she was left home alone. She doesn't listen. I received the news via FaceTime at work. To say that I was happy, would be an understatement. I didn't give a damn how I found out. All that mattered to me was that I was going to be a daddy. That was the longest 8-hour shift that I ever worked. I couldn't wait to get home to celebrate with my baby's mama.

The days that followed were some of our happiest. We couldn't stop talking about the baby. I was calling it a boy, trying to speak it into existence. We spent all of our time debating names, picking out clothes, and preparing for our new addition. We told

Charleigh, and our families the great news. Everyone was so excited for us.

I've been waiting a long time to be a Pop. (Well, since I've been with Al, before then I was trying to avoid becoming one at all costs.) I was ready to have someone call me Daddy. I wasn't scared at all. I felt prepared. I was ecstatic. I was finally going to be able to put all of these years of studying my Pops, Uncle Phil and James Evans to use. I was ready to embrace my new title of Father.

Unfortunately, less than two weeks later, we found out that we were having a miscarriage. Something that I now know is extremely common. This was devastating news. We've been praying and hoping for this gift for so long. We finally get it, and just like that, all of our excitement is snatched away from us.

I was hurt, but I knew that it was time to go into support mode. I knew that Al needed me. We were both very confused and upset, but it is my job to console her. I'm not sure how good of a job that I did, but I tried. I didn't have much to say. There was nothing that she could hear from me that would make this situation better. All that I could do was pray. I didn't ask why. I only asked for peace. I trust God. Always. In the good times, and in between them.

Life isn't fair, but life isn't over. I know that one day soon, I will see that smile on Al's tear covered face again. I know that we will have our baby (boy). And one day I will try my best to be the greatest daddy of all time. Until then, we will just have to enjoy trying. I ain't mad at that.

4.14.16

Stay True.

"With the first pick in the 1996 NBA Draft, the Philadelphia 76ers select...Allen Iverson from Georgetown University."

When AI came into the league in 96, it changed everything. In my eyes, he changed the world. He was unlike anybody that the association had ever seen. He was a different animal. He made it clear early in his career that he was here to change the game.

I never wanted to be like Mike, but if I did, that would've changed the night that AI crossed him, lost him, and knocked down the jumper at the top of the key. That one play displays everything that I, and most of my generation love about The Answer. He was fearless. Here he was, a young rookie, trying to make a name for himself. He had only been in the league for a few months when the reigning king of the NBA switched on to him. He didn't shy away from the challenge. He knew that nobody in the world could hold him. Including the arguable G.O.A.T. He attacked, and his legacy began.

Throughout his career, AI continued to play the same way. With absolutely zero fear. He went at any and everybody that dared to get in a defensive stance in front of him. He was in attack mode from the tip off until the clock read all zeros. He would receive criticism for not passing the ball enough, for not being coachable, and for his practice habits. (yes, we talking about practice.) But I didn't care about any of that, what I saw was the smallest guy on the court, at only 6 feet tall and 165 pounds on his tippy toes and soaking wet, having the biggest impact. Killing guards out on the perimeter and absorbing punishment from the giants in the paint. They could knock him down ten times in a row, he wouldn't stop coming. By the end of the game he would have another 40 ball, a W, and the respect of everybody in the arena.

Off the court, he shined just as bright. He didn't conform to what people expected a professional athlete to be. He was a true original. He was the first superstar in the NBA to wear cornrows and to be covered in tattoos. He paved the way for athletes today when self expression was extremely unpopular and highly ridiculed. He never forgot where he came from. He always showed love and gave back. He never switched up. Some people hated him, others loved him, it really didn't matter. He was always himself. Regardless.

He was so genuine. This is what drew people to him. I've never seen an athlete have as much influence on culture. Young black culture in particular. Every black boy that I knew wanted to be like him, and every black woman, young and old, was crushing on him. Damn near every kid in my school had cornrows, male and female. Boys that couldn't even dribble a basketball were wearing sleeves on their arms with matching headbands. Girls had on Philly jersey dresses with matching Reebok Questions. What a time.

He had so much influence that even his peers started dressing like him. Pre-game would look like a video shoot. Big chains, du-rags, earrings and three sizes too large throwback jerseys. Some guys looked like clowns, it was obvious that they were only imitating greatness, it wasn't authentic. The league would eventually implement a dress code, citing the need for a more "professional" look. I'm sure that they didn't like AI being the face of the previously clean-cut NBA. They were trying to rein him in. His shirt size might've lost one or two Xs before the L, but they couldn't change who he was, or what he meant to the people.

"With the 13th pick in the 1996 NBA Draft, the Charlotte Hornets select...Kobe Bryant from Lower Merion High School in Pennsylvania."

Kobe Bryant came into the league as a 17 year-old kid. As the first guard drafted into the NBA from high school, many "experts" doubted his game. He didn't care. He had supreme confidence. Not only did he want to be the greatest of all time, he actually believed that he could.

Kobe did not set the league on fire right out of the gate. He was not in the starting lineup for the Lakers (who he was traded to on draft night). He played about 16 minutes and averaged 8 points a game. But when he was on the court, in his mind, he was the best player out there.

In Game 5 of the '97 Western Conference Semifinals, the Lakers were facing elimination against the Utah Jazz. Their superstar center, and go to guy, Shaq fouled out. Young Kobe thought that it was his time to shine, time to launch his legacy. With his sky high confidence, Kobe naturally wanted the ball in his hands. He got his wish. He rose up for four jumpers in the last 5 minutes. All air balls. The Utah fans were killing him, laughing, booing, and calling him all types of ball hogs. Some of his teammates were agreeing with the fans in their heads. The announcers explained how this would destroy his confidence.

They didn't know who they were talking about. They also didn't account for his work ethic that was greater than his confidence. For the next twenty years, he worked his way to greatness. He was obsessed. He wasn't the most loved player in the NBA, by his teammates, opponents, or fans outside of Los Angeles (he's a god in Los Angeles.) He wasn't looking to be liked, he wanted to be great.

He had many critics, he was often accused of separating himself, being too demanding, running teammates out of town, and of course, shooting the ball too much. He paid the naysayers no attention and played his game. It was the only way he knew how to get the job done. His system earned him five championships, countless awards and records, and put him in the conversation as the greatest ever as he announced that his twentieth season would be his last.

The past two weeks, I have been in basketball heaven. March Madness just ended with a great final game. The NBA season just ended, the playoffs are now set to begin. These are things that I look forward to every year, but this year was special.

Last Saturday, Allen Iverson was announced as a first ballot hall of famer, the biggest honor in basketball. In a great HOF class, he received the most love. His impact has been undeniable and he is finally being recognized for it. The inductees were set to be acknowledged on the court and in front of the world on Final Four Saturday. The rest of the inductees all had on suits, looking like they had an interview for a promotion at work. Not my man AI, that's not what got him to this point. He has never been one to fit in. There he was, receiving the highest honor in his field, in true Answer fashion. Fitted hat, tee, jeans and gold chains. Real AI. Still AI.

Last night, I witnessed one of the greatest feats that I have ever seen on a basketball court. Kobe's farewell season has been a tough one. The Lakers are far from the championship franchise that they once were. They are in last place and have been out of the playoff race since training camp. Kobe has been celebrated all year long, and for his final game, all eyes were on him. The opponent? The Utah Jazz of all teams. This matchup would end a lot differently than their playoff game 20 years prior. Kobe didn't disappoint. The whole game, the world wanted him to do what he was most known and criticized for his entire career, shoot the ball. And that he did, fifty times. No one was mad about it. He ended the game with 60 points, and single-handedly willed the Lakers to a comeback victory. I couldn't believe what I was watching as the shots kept falling. The Staples Center crowd and the whole world online was chanting his name. Hollywood couldn't script a better ending.

I've learned so much from the game of basketball. Lessons that I apply to my everyday life and will carry with me forever. In the past two weeks, I have learned a very simple lesson from two greats. Believe in yourself and stay true, even when it is not the popular choice. It doesn't matter if people agree or disagree, love or hate you. It's your life, you might as well live it how you want. You have to do what feels right to you. You might end up being celebrated for it. If not, who cares? Celebrate your damn self.

5.1.16

Fix.

I went back to Kansas City two weeks ago. I had the honor of being a groomsman for one of my close friend's. I was happy to make the trip and help my boy celebrate. I wasn't happy with the size of the pants of the rented tux, but it wasn't about me.

I was just home for Thanksgiving, but for some reason, that felt like so long ago. The days leading up to the trip, I felt anxious, I was ready to go. I couldn't wait to get back. I needed to feel the energy of the city. Something about going home always makes me feel rejuvenated. I go home for a few days, get my Kansas City fix and go on about my business back in reality. When this visit was over, I felt no different.

I spent the majority of my time with my parents. They live across town from each other, so I was making a lot of trips back and forth. They are both dealing with health issues. I was happy to do whatever I could to make them feel a little better while I was in the city. Which most of the time meant just hanging at the house laughing and joking with them or praying with them, or listening to words of wisdom, or laying in the bed with them, or taking them to get something to eat. I would have cooked for them, but I'm not trying to kill them. I can't throw down worth shit in the kitchen. I just wanted to be in their presence as much as possible.

Other times when I have come home, I couldn't wait to be in the streets. As soon as I would touch down in the city, I was on the move. I needed to hit all the spots, be on the scene. This visit, I was happy being wherever they were. I was not able to see everybody that I wanted to, or that wanted to see me, but I felt like spending time with them was more important.

When I wasn't with them, I was with my other family, my friends. It's crazy to see where we are now. Time is passing so fast. It seems like only yesterday we were giving teacher's hell, getting kicked out of classrooms or fighting and tearing shit up and getting kicked out of clubs. Now most of my boys are fathers, some are husbands, all of them are good ass people. We all have responsibilities these days, and take care of them, but when we get together, we still ain't shit. Just how I like it.

Son and friend are two roles that I take very serious. Sometimes, I question myself if I'm being the best that I can be. I left Kansas City in 2011, I needed to explore, I was looking for excitement. It was very necessary. In the almost 5 years since I left, I have had a lot of great experiences and met a lot of great people, including my soon to be wife. I know that I made the right decision when I left, but lately, I've been missing home a lot more. I feel guilty not being there for my parents. I wish that I was closer to my boy's and their families. I don't long for excitement as much as I used to. I find happiness just being with people that I love and that I know love me.

I'm blessed that whenever I go home, nothing has changed. Despite the gaps between my visits, the connection is still there. This and the support that I receive from my people back home and my family out here make me want to be great. I know that I will only be as strong as the people in my life. If I can have half of the strength of the people that made me, I'll be alright. They make my life better, I hope that I do the same for them.

I often think about moving the family from Maryland back to Kansas City. The primary motivation for this is me missing my family. That's not a good enough reason. For one, my mother would be pissed if I was there just looking her in the face every day. She would kick me out after a week. I've got business to take care of and work to do. Right now, I am exactly where I need to be. Doing what I need to do, and making them proud, is more important than my family seeing me every day. So, until I need my next hit of home, I'll be here in the DMV handling business, trying to put on for my people.

5.3.16

We ain't getting no younger, we might as well do it.

I've known that I was going to marry Alex since July 2013. The first time that I saw her coming out of LAX, I knew it. Well, I knew that I was supposed to, I wasn't sure if she was going to let me. As soon as I saw her walk out of the airport doors, it was a wrap. I wasn't ready to be a husband, hell, I wasn't even ready to be a boyfriend, but I knew that one day if she didn't mind putting up with my crazy ass, she would be my wife.

I guess she doesn't mind. Almost three years later, she's still here. We've been through so much and have grown together. Neither of us were prepared to be married when we first decided to give this a shot. We just knew that we wanted to ride together and see where this road would take us. She didn't know that she was getting in an old Cadillac with a broken passenger door that only opens from the outside. In other words, her ass is stuck on this ride. In too deep.

We're very nontraditional. We openly discussed marriage often. We both knew that it was what we wanted. Charleigh would ask me once a week when were we getting married. She wants a little brother or sister and thinks that marriage will automatically make that happen. I hope she's right. I always would tell her "soon." One day, Alex and I decided that we were ready. We said it's time, let's set a date. "We ain't gettin no younger, we might as well do it." We agreed on the day and location, she bought her dress that she had been looking at for about a year now, and we told our family and friends to save the date. Only one thing was missing, the ring on her finger.

I'm big on making memories. Alex, not so much. She has made it clear to me over the years, that she does not want a big extravagant proposal. And even though we had already decided that we wanted to get married, I still wanted to make a memory of the moment that I asked her to be my wife.

I got the ring that she wanted. I knew what she wanted because she's been showing me rings since we first started dating, she made it easy for me. I ain't got time to get some mystery ring that she doesn't like and doesn't want to wear. I wanted her to love what I was asking her to wear every day for the rest of her life to let guys know to leave her the hell alone. Now, I just had to figure out how I wanted to ask her to wear it proudly and be my wife.

We were planning on going back to Kansas City together for a weekend. I thought, perfect, we can make a memory in my hometown. I was going to take her to our favorite museum back home, to have a picnic on the lawn, it's a beautiful location. I was going to have a photographer set up in the cut to take pictures of me on one knee. It was going to be a good memory. However, like the great prophet Andre 3000 said, "You can plan a pretty picnic, but you can't predict the weather." Alex wasn't feeling good and had a lot of work and travel coming up, so she couldn't make the trip back to KC with me. Plans ruined.

Now I had no plan, and the clock was ticking. She told me that she wasn't going on the trip on Tuesday and I was flying out Friday morning. She would be working in California when I got back so we would be apart for almost two weeks. I needed this ring on her finger before I left. Thursday rolled around, and I still couldn't come up with a plan. I decided to do something that I personally think I'm great at, wing it.

Thursday is our date night every week, I knew that by the end of the evening I had to pop the question that I already had the answer to, but I didn't know how. I had the ring in my pocket and was waiting for the right moment. We went on our date and had a great time. We went to a nice restaurant and had a nice booth that looked setup for a proposal. I knew that Alex would be embarrassed and pissed if I dropped down to one knee in front of all these people. So, it didn't happen there. Next thing I knew, we were back at home, the ring still in my pocket. The clock was ticking.

We were in the bed listening to some of our favorite songs that tell our story over the last three years. We were feeling great, we were in our element, laughing, kissing, enjoying each other. While I was singing to her, I took the ring out of my pocket and placed it in her hand. She asked "what the hell is that?" with a look on her face that I'll never forget. She knew what the hell it was, and she was ready for it. I slid off the bed, onto one knee. I grabbed her hand and looked her in the eye and asked "You really fuck with me, huh? You really love me?" She said yes, I told her, "I love you too, more than anything in the world, will you be my wife?" She said, "YES." with the biggest grin I've ever seen on her face. Mission complete. Memory made.

5.21.16

N-I-G-G-A.

One of my best friends growing up was a kid named Collin. When I was about 9 years old, one day, he just showed up at my doorstep. He knocked on my door on a Friday night. I remember because I was watching Family Matters. TGIF. My big brother opened the door, and there stood a little white boy. He asked, "Is it a kid here that plays ball?" He saw my goal outside and wanted some action. My brother laughed and called me from the back. He told me that a kid came to challenge me. I threw my shoes on, ready to give out some buckets. Ain't no way somebody was gonna come to my home court and beat me. That's what I thought. I was wrong.

It was a good game, but he beat me. And talked shit while he did it. I liked him. From that day forward, we were tight.

We went to different schools, but we hung out every day. Playing ball, talking shit, getting into trouble, watching wrestling, playing video games. Regular kid stuff. That was my dawg. He was a cool ass kid. He wasn't trying to be black, but all of his friends were black, so he had soul. He stayed in the freshest jerseys and shoes, and always had the new music.

In the mid-90's, my mother was heavy in the church. She didn't allow "worldly" music in the house. Collin's mom let us listen to whatever (Rest well, Ms. Sherri). While I was over there, I would catch up on everything that I was missing out on. My favorites were Bone Thugs "E.1999 Eternal", BIG's "Ready to Die" and "All Eyez on Me" by Tupac.

All Eyez on Me is a masterpiece. I knew this when I was 9 years old. This statement is still true 20 years later. I didn't know back then how powerful Pac was, or how much I would look up to him. All I knew was that his music jammed. I didn't understand what he was talking about most of the time, I didn't need to. I felt it. My favorite song on the album was "Ratha Be Ya Nigga".

"I don't wanna be yo man, I wanna be yo nigga."

When I was 9, I wasn't anybody's man, or nigga, but the song was still my shit. Once I finally got old enough to deal with women, and I knew exactly what Pac was saying, I took the same stance.

I loved women. I enjoyed being in their company. I wanted to spend as much time with as many women as possible. A commitment was the last thing on my mind. I didn't want to be their man, I was trying to be their nigga.

I was a good nigga. I flourished in the role. One thing that I wasn't, was a player. I wasn't trying to trick anybody into dealing with me. I didn't run game. I didn't sell dreams. I developed a pattern. I would meet a new young lady, (well, some weren't that young, I had a few vets) and we would hit it off. Very early into us getting to know each other, past relationships would come up. I would explain that I've never been in a committed relationship and didn't want to be. I would put the ball in her court. She knew exactly where I stood. More often than not, for whatever reason, she would be okay with that, and we would continue doing what we were doing.

"We can get drunk and smoke weed all day."

These situationships were filled with good times. We didn't get drunk and smoke weed all day, but we would indulge occasionally. We were just kicking it. Nothing serious. We had an understanding. While I'm with you, we'll have a good time, when I'm not, don't ask me any questions. This would usually last for about a month or two. Feelings were often caught, and I would start receiving questions. "What are we?" "How long are we going to keep doing this?" "When are we going to take the next step?"

I don't wanna be yo man, I wanna be yo nigga.

This was the pattern for years. I had a lot of fun, but no real connections. No substance. I wasn't looking for substance anyway, I was content.

This was the case until I met my match. When we first start dealing with one another, I told Alex what I had told every woman before her, that I wasn't looking for a relationship. We were long distance for the first six months anyway, so this really wasn't an issue. We developed a great friendship and foundation before we ever touched. After spending one day with her in person, I wanted nothing more than to be in a relationship with her.

I can't really explain why everything changed for me. I guess that I just met the right woman at the right time. As soon as I saw her, a switch went off. It was time to grow up. I didn't want to be her nigga, I wanted to be her man. Now, I am preparing myself to be her husband. I've come a long way. I'd like to think that if Pac would've never been taken away from us, he would've changed his tune too. I enjoyed being a nigga, but I take more pride in being a man.

I know that we talk a lot about the future, but I thank you for where I am today.

5.28.16

Countdown.

Today was my last full day as a single man. The weeks have been
flying by ever since we became engaged. The time is finally here. I
should probably be sleeping right now, but I guess that I'm too
excited.

Alex and I decided to go our separate ways for these last 24 hours
until it is time to exchange our vows tomorrow evening. Our
original plan was to have no contact with each other, but as soon
as she went out with her homegirls and got a little liquor in her
system, I started receiving texts. "Are we really doing this?" "Am I
really going to be your wife?" "Are we really getting married
tomorrow?" Yes. Yes. Yes. This is not a drill, the shit is real. I was
waiting for her to contact me, I knew that we couldn't go that long
without communication, unless I'm in the doghouse. I probably
could've gone about another hour before I would've reached out. I
was missing her.

Some of my people are in town for the festivities. We decided to
keep the wedding small. If we wanted to open it up, all of Kansas
City would've invaded DC, but we decided against that. We
wanted to keep it simple, some of our closest friends and family

made the trip. I kicked it with my boys tonight. We just got back in the house at almost 4 AM. I haven't been in the streets that late in years. I'm old. I can't hang like I used to.

For the last month, the fellas have been asking me what the plan was for the night before the wedding. I've never enjoyed being the center of attention, so I hate being put in these situations. I don't have parties for my birthday for the same reason. They wanted to know what was up with the bachelor party. I told them that we would get out and have a good time, but it wouldn't be anything crazy. The last 15 years of my life have been a bachelor party, I didn't need one more night to cap it off. I already put my time in. My bachelor days are certified, the only thing left for me to do is have my jersey raised to the rafters.

Since I vetoed the strip club, or anything else that involved tipping strangers (I'm cheap). We really didn't have a plan, and I was cool with that. Since they came all the way to DC to celebrate with me, I wanted everybody to have a good time. We went out to a couple of bars, hit the streets a little bit, let them feel the vibe of the district.

The whole night, I couldn't even focus on kicking it. All I could think about was the step that we are taking tomorrow. Even though I swore up and down that I would never get married, (Not for nothin, never happen, I'll be forever mackin.) I knew deep down that one day, I would be taking the plunge. The day is finally here. It is after midnight, it is now May 28th. The biggest day of my life.

When I looked at my phone and saw the date, it felt like time froze. It's not many dates that I know that I will remember forever, but this is one of them. Today is the day that I step up to the plate. I am putting it all on the line. I am betting on myself. We are betting on each other.

I hear a lot of people bash marriage, understandably so. They can get ugly, it doesn't seem to be too many success stories these days. But, we aren't afraid. I am going into this with high hopes and higher expectations. I know who I am marrying. I know where her heart is. I also knew who I am. I know who I need to be and what I need to do make this marriage successful. That is exactly what I am going to do. We are in control of our marriage, nobody else. We will protect it at all costs. We will not let anything threaten our union. It is a treasure, and we will protect it as such.

I'm so excited. I can not wait until I see my beautiful bride tomorrow. I am not second guessing the decision at all. I'm ready. 14 hours to go.

I woke up this morning with fire in my eyes, love in my heart, and peace in my mind. Thank you.

5.28.16

Exchange.

When I woke up, I knew that it would be a huge day, but I didn't know what to expect. This is the biggest day of my life. I am making the most important decision that I've ever made. How do I prepare myself for this? Do I even try to prepare myself? Do I go with the flow? I've never gotten married before. I'm not true to this, I'm new to this. I decided to go with what has gotten me this far, winging it. Whatever is going to happen, will happen. I decided to just embrace everything as it came and enjoy the day.

I was not nervous. I was not afraid. My feet weren't cold at all. I was ready. I wasn't under any pressure. This is exactly what I wanted to do, when I wanted to do it. It was time to take the next step. The only thing that I was slightly worried about was delivering my vows.

We decided to write our own. The pressure was on. I was brainstorming for weeks. I had to recite my vows after Maya Angelou Jr. Great. My bride has literally written books of love notes. I was outmatched. I decided to stop stressing, and just write down what I promise to do as a husband. I was proud when I finished them. I let mom hear what I came up with, she approved.

I was set. The hours leading up to the ceremony went by so fast. It felt like I woke up, blinked, and was standing in front of the Reverend in my suit, (cleaner than an a deacon on Easter Sunday) waiting for Alex to join me, so we could get the party started.

And there she was, walking towards me. So beautiful. Tears flowing down her cheeks. I was hoping that they were tears of joy. People had been asking me all week if I was going to cry. I had no clue. If I felt the tears coming, I wouldn't hold back, but I wasn't planning on needing any kleenex. It was a happy day, and I usually only shed tears on sad occasions. I was elated. No tears were on my face, only a big, picture day smile.

The Rev was performing a grand ceremony. Al delivered beautiful, heartfelt vows, like I knew that she would, and now it was time for me to handle my business. I cleared my throat, it was showtime...

I commit my body and heart to you, to be yours and only yours.

I vow to stand by your side, through the peaks and valleys of this life. To laugh, cry, and grow with you. To pray for you, and with you. To share the joy of the good days, and comfort you through the hard nights.

I vow to protect and provide for our household. To lead our family and support your dreams.

You are a blessing and my best friend. I vow to treat you as such, with loyalty, trust, honor and respect. Above all, I vow to love you, as you are, unconditionally and without hesitation. Always.

My job for the day was done. The bride was kissed. Mr. and Mrs. Spearman were presented.

The rest of the night was a blur. We had a great time with our friends and family. We laughed, cried (Mama's speech got me), and danced the night away. Now, we are in bed as Husband and Wife. The day was a success. We were already out here. Now, we are really out here.

5.29.16

Pressure Makes Diamonds.

I woke up this morning next to my wife. That is crazy for me to say. My wife. I spent the first moments of my day just staring at her in disbelief. I can't believe that I am a married man. I am in awe of the fact that we finally started our marathon.

I wasn't always sure that we would make it to this point. We had to fight, pray, and work to get here. If this wasn't exactly what we wanted, if we didn't share the same common goal, there is no way that our dream would now be a reality.

The three years that we have been together have been anything but uneventful. I have experienced my highest highs, and had some of my best times. I also had to work harder on myself than ever before.

I've been on my own for the most part since I was 18. I did what I wanted, when I wanted, how I wanted. I thought that paying bills and making my own decisions made me a man. Doing these things made me feel like an adult, but it wasn't until I said, "I do." and meant it, that I knew for a fact that I was a man.

I know this because I was tested. Marriage has always been the goal for myself concerning Alex. We've talked about it since we first started our relationship. I remember looking for rings and making plans to go to the courthouse as soon as we lived together while we were still long distance. We knew that we loved each other, and felt like that was all that we needed. We thought that everything else would just fall into place.

We were completely head over heels. But, I didn't want to rush into marriage, neither of us did. We both understood how serious that commitment is. We decided that living together, or shacking up, as the church folks call it, would be the best next step for us.

Living together was our training camp. We were both pushed to our limits. Our love was challenged. There were times that we both wanted to call it quits. Times that we doubted ourselves. Times where we doubted each other. But, we always bounced back. We learned so much. Individually and collectively. I made plenty of mistakes, spent plenty of night in the doghouse. I'm not perfect, no where near it, but she never gave up on me. Never gave up on us. She pissed me off many times. There were days that I didn't want anything to do with her. But I still kept my faith in her. Kept my faith in us. And now we're here.

I know for a fact that being married is a part of my purpose. It is a must that I be the best man that I can be. To be the best possible version of myself. Being a husband gives me new responsibility, a greater sense of accountability. As the head of a household, and the leader of a family, failure isn't an option. Now I have people depending on me. If I don't reach my potential, we all suffer. It is pressure on me now, but I've never been one to shy away from that. If it's a big shot to take, I want the ball in my hands. Pressure bursts pipes, that scares some people. But pressure also makes diamonds, and I am ready to shine.

I woke up this morning feeling better than ever. For the first time in a long time, I feel like I am exactly where I need to be, when I need to be there. I know that this journey won't be easy. However, I'm gonna take it one step at a time and attack each day like it's my last. The possibilities are endless.

When I started this journey, I wanted to live in a kingly manner. I wanted more for myself. Laying in the bed this morning, with my Queen's head resting on my chest, I feel that I have accomplished just that. I look down and see the ring on my finger, it feels like I have a crown on my head. I will hold my head high and be the man that I was made to be.

A real king doesn't fall in love, he stands up in it.

Bonus.

6.11.16

Ode to Ali II.

Last Friday I heard the reports. You had been placed on life
support. The family was with you, this was looking like the end.
My heart dropped. I knew that you were in the hospital, but the
reports weren't that it was life threatening until today.

Selfishly, I wanted this to just be another victory after you were
given no chance. I wanted you to shake up the world again. Like
when you beat Liston in '64, Foreman in '74, or Spinks in '78. If
anybody could do it, you could. You're the champ. The Greatest.
But, now wasn't the time for me to be selfish. Especially with you,
you've been the definition of selfless for over 50 years.

I said a prayer. I prayed that God's will would be done. That if you
were ready to rest, that you could rest peacefully. Your daughter
shared the story of your heart beating for thirty minutes after your
organs shut down. The doctors had never seen that before. That's
the true heart of a champion.

Word spread of your passing fast. Love poured in from all over the world. Everyone mourned the death of The People's Champ. On the day of your memorial, all eyes were on Louisville, KY, your home town. The streets were filled with thousands of people wanting to pay their respects and say their goodbyes. Ali! Ali! Ali! Is all that you heard. You touched so many lives all around the globe, including mine.

I've learned many lessons from watching and studying your life throughout the years. I'm still learning from you, even in death. The world will never stop chanting your name. All because you dared to be great. You knew your purpose and became it. In a world that discourages black men from being great, you accepted every challenge to become The Greatest. While doing so, you inspired millions to do the same. You showed us all that impossible is nothing, that greatness is achievable.

You were so many things, words can't capture you. Simply put, you truly were The Greatest, a true King. Kings never die. Your impact will be felt forever. Your presence on earth was a gift. Thank you. Rest well, Champ. You deserve it. Job well done.

Young Man, Rumble

Ryan Spear